W9-BTJ-501

HOME REPAIR AND IMPROVEMENT

CLEANING

TIME®
LIFE
BOOKS

TX
324

OTHER PUBLICATIONS:

DO IT YOURSELF
The Time-Life Complete Gardener
Home Repair and Improvement
The Art of Woodworking
Fix It Yourself

COOKING
Weight Watchers® Smart Choice Recipe Collection
Great Taste/Low Fat
Williams-Sonoma Kitchen Library

HISTORY
The American Story
Voices of the Civil War
The American Indians
Lost Civilizations
Mysteries of the Unknown
Time Frame
The Civil War
Cultural Atlas

TIME-LIFE KIDS
Family Time Bible Stories
Library of First Questions and Answers
A Child's First Library of Learning
I Love Math
Nature Company Discoveries
Understanding Science & Nature

SCIENCE/NATURE
Voyage Through the Universe

For information on and a full description
of any of the Time-Life Books series listed above,
please call 1-800-621-7026 or write:

Reader Information
Time-Life Customer Service
P.O. Box C-32068
Richmond Virginia 23261-2068

HOME REPAIR AND IMPROVEMENT

CLEANING

BY THE EDITORS OF TIME-LIFE BOOKS, ALEXANDRIA, VIRGINIA

The Consultants

Mark Browning is Vice-President and Director of Varsity Contractors Inc., a cleaning company in Pocatello, Idaho. He has more than 30 years of experience in the cleaning and maintenance industry. As a partner in Aslett-Browning Inc., he has been instrumental in publishing many cleaning books including *Cleaning Up for a Living*, *The Cleaning Encyclopedia*, *Pet Cleanup Made Easy*, and *The Stain Buster's Bible*. He currently serves as a committee member for the Building Services Contractors Association International.

Dr. Richard D. Kramer holds a PhD in Entomology and is the president of Innovative Pest Management Inc., located in Olney, Maryland. He serves as the Contributing Technical Editor and columnist for *Service Technician* and *Pest Control Technology* magazines. He was the Director of Research, Education and Technical Resources for the National Pest Control Association from 1991 to 1996. Dr. Kramer is a Board-Certified Entomologist and a member of the Entomological Society of America.

Mike Staats is the operations manager of Staats Services Today, an appliance repair company in Peoria, Illinois. He has 32 years of experience with major appliance sales and repair, and has been an appliance repair instructor in the Peoria Park District continuing education program. Mr. Staats is the host of the nationally syndicated radio program "The Repair Show with Captain Toolhead" and is a consultant to the *Family Handyman Magazine* on major appliances.

Jacqueline Stephens and Jane Rising both hold positions at the International Fabricare Institute in Silver Spring, Maryland. Jacqueline Stephens, with a BSc in Textile Management Technology, is the Director of Garment Analysis. Jane Rising holds a degree in Home Economics and is an instructor of dry cleaning and stain removal in the Education Department. Both are popular industry speakers and have written numerous articles and bulletins for *Fabricare* magazine.

CONTENTS

1 A CLEANER AND METHOD FOR EVERY OCCASION   6

A Battery of Cleaning Products   8

An Arsenal of Cleaning Tools   11

Reviving Wood Finishes   13

Caring for Wood Floors   16

Tending to Wickerwork   19

Removing Grime from Masonry   20

Blasting Off Dirt with Water   26

Rejuvenating Metal   29

Keeping Up the Appearance of Plastics   33

Cleaning Glass   37

Shining Up Porcelain and Tile   40

Brightening Walls and Ceilings   42

2 CARING FOR TEXTILES   44

A Methodical Approach to Removing Spots   46

Rejuvenating Rugs and Carpets   52

Lifting Soil from Upholstery   59

3 SPECIAL CLEANING PROBLEMS   62

Taking Care of Household Appliances   64

Attending to Air Filters   75

Keeping Swimming Pools Clean and Clear   79

Dealing with the Aftermath of a Flood   84

4 CONTROLLING HOUSEHOLD PESTS   92

Pestproofing a House   94

Taking Offensive Action   100

A Guide to Common Pests   105

5 APPENDIX   112

Cleaning Hardwood Floors   113

Restoring Metal Surfaces   114

Caring for Fabrics   116

Cures for Stained Textiles   118

Treating Swimming-Pool Water   122

Choosing Pesticides   124

Index   126

Acknowledgments   128

Picture Credits   128

1
A Cleaner and Method for Every Occasion

Homeowners who would never fix a faucet or rewire a light switch without a well-stocked toolbox and clear directions routinely embark on cleaning projects with little guidance or preparation. Most homes contain an astonishing variety of materials, including wood, vinyl, porcelain, and glass. Each one is best cleaned with a particular tool, method, and cleaning product.

A Battery of Cleaning Products   8

An Arsenal of Cleaning Tools   11

Reviving Wood Finishes   13

Scrubbing Down Wood Siding

Caring for Wood Floors   16

Refinishing a Small Area
Stripping and Rewaxing a Floor

Tending to Wickerwork   19

Removing Grime from Masonry   20

Dislodging Surface Deposits
Restoring the Glow of Dressed Stone
Applying a Protective Sealer
Coating an Asphalt Driveway

Blasting Off Dirt with Water   26

Power-Washing an Exterior Wall

Rejuvenating Metal   29

Bringing Back the Gleam of Brass
Polishing Silver
Scrubbing Grime off Metal Blinds
Brushing Away Rust and Dirt
Sandblasting Metalwork

Keeping Up the Appearance of Plastics   33

Recoating Vinyl Floors
Polishing an Acrylic Storm Window
Remedies for Damaged Countertops

Cleaning Glass   37

Washing Windows with a Squeegee
Making Chandeliers Sparkle

Shining Up Porcelain and Tile   40

Caring for Grout

Brightening Walls and Ceilings   42

Scrubbing grout with a special brush →

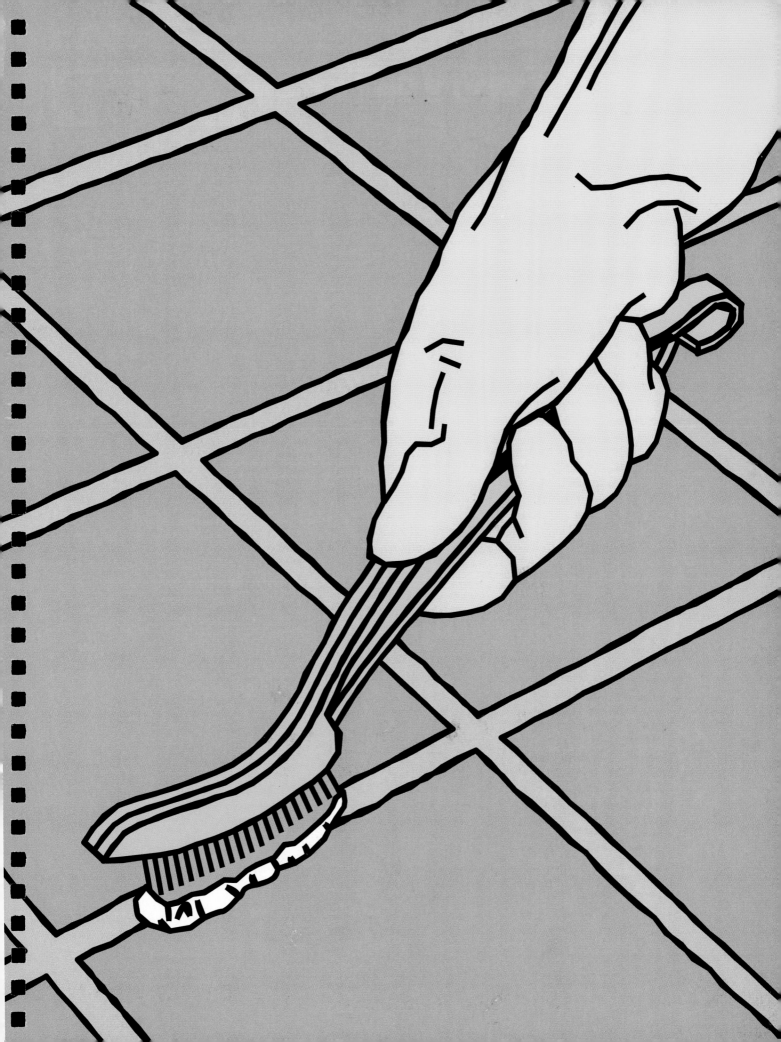

A Battery of Cleaning Products

Most cleaners fall into five general categories based on similarity of function. A few special cleaners, however, are one of a kind, designed to solve individual problems *(opposite)*.

Abrasives: Gritty compounds containing mineral particles, abrasives are sometimes mixed with detergent, bleach, or other substances. Suitable for cleaning and polishing metals, they are often present in scouring powders for cleaning and brightening surfaces such as ceramic tile and porcelain plumbing fixtures.

Abrasives work by dislodging dirt, then the detergent in the mixture lifts the dirt particles from the surface. Use care when cleaning plastic, fiberglass, imitation marble, or chrome with abrasives—some can dull the surface permanently.

Absorbents: These powdered substances soak up fresh spills from porous materials. Cornmeal, cornstarch, salt, and talcum powder are excellent all-purpose absorbents; clay-base cat litter is good for drawing oil from stained asphalt and concrete.

Bleaches: Containing chlorine, hydrogen peroxide, sodium perborate, or sodium percarbonate, bleaches are designed to clean, brighten, and deodorize. Chlorine bleach also disinfects and can remove stains from sinks, tubs, and tiles; lighten dark or discolored wood; disinfect swimming pools; and strip mildew from exterior wood or masonry.

Solvents: These products dissolve soil without water. Perchloroethylene (PERC), a staple in commercial dry cleaning, is available for home use to remove stains from fabrics. Orange oil dissolves grease and gummy residues left by tape and chewing gum. Other solvents include mineral spirits and paint removers.

Detergents: These synthetic substitutes for soap work by breaking up and dispersing soil particles so they can be rinsed away. The most common detergents are a mild liquid for dishwashing and the general-purpose household type, sold in powder or liquid form. In addition, a liquid glass cleaner comes in handy; for tough jobs you'll need a heavy-duty degreaser (available as a spray or as a concentrate from janitorial supply stores). Automatic dishwasher detergent—$\frac{1}{2}$ cup diluted in 1 gallon of water—serves as an effective degreaser.

If your household includes children or anyone vulnerable to infection, you may want a disinfectant cleaner for the bathroom and sick rooms.

MAKING ENVIRONMENTALLY SOUND CHOICES

To protect the environment, choose and use cleaning products with care.

✔ Buy only as much of a product as you need for the job.

✔ Use products with phosphates only if your municipal water-treatment system has a phosphorus-removal process.

✔ Choose water-base cleaners over solvent-base ones when possible, and avoid environmentally hostile chemicals when there is a practical alternative.

✔ Pass any leftover products to a neighbor rather than throwing them away.

✔ Flush water-base cleaners down the drain, but never pour them on the ground or down a storm sewer, and avoid dumping large quantities of any cleaning product into a septic system. Dispose of solvents and other nonwater-base substances through a municipal hazardous waste-disposal program.

✔ Purchase cleaners in concentrated form to cut down on packaging.

✔ Rinse containers that held water-soluble liquids thoroughly before throwing them away; shake out dry products. Recycle the containers when possible.

SPECIAL CLEANERS

Cleaning agent	Applications	Cautions and dilutions	Sources
Acetone	Removes varnish, lacquer, nail polish, and airplane glue from natural fibers, wood, tile, and vinyl.	Do not use on acetate, triacetate, or modacrylic fibers. Do not dilute.	Drugstores, hardware stores
Isopropyl alcohol	Disinfects; used in poultices to draw stains out of masonry.	Available full strength, or in 70% solution sold as rubbing alcohol.	Paint stores, drug stores, supermarkets
Ammonia	Cleans stains from ceramic tile and nonaluminum cookware; removes perspiration, urine, and grease from fabrics. Cuts grease and grime on appliances.	Use at full strength for stain removal. Mix $\frac{1}{2}$ cup in a gallon of water for cleaning appliances; do not apply to aluminum or painted surfaces.	Drugstores, supermarkets
Muriatic acid	Removes efflorescence from concrete and stains from concrete swimming pools.	When used on concrete, dilute with 10 parts water; on swimming pools, dilute with 4 parts water.	Hardware stores
Oxalic acid	Removes most inks from fabrics and wood floors; rust and copper stains from porcelain bathtubs and sinks; rust from masonry and stone.	For fabrics or wood floors, dilute 1 tablespoon in 2 cups water; for porcelain, masonry, or stone, dilute 1 part in 20 parts water.	Drugstores

Deploying specialty cleaners.
Each of the cleaning agents in this chart, listed by its common name, has specific applications. Many of them require special safety precautions *(page 10)*. Some are powerful enough to damage certain surfaces if used at full strength—remember to dilute them when necessary. Before using any of these chemicals, read and follow the package directions, and test the product first on an inconspicuous area of the material being cleaned. All of the chemicals may be purchased in generic form; they are also available as active ingredients in brand-name products.

VINEGAR AND BAKING SODA: SAFE AND CONVENIENT

A variety of light cleaning tasks can be accomplished with the ordinary household products vinegar and baking soda. Although you may need to clean more often and use more elbow grease than with many commercial products—and will still need a disinfectant when one is called for—they are safer for human health and the environment.

Plain white vinegar contains a mild acid called acetic acid. Diluted in water, vinegar removes perspiration, urine, and metallic stains from natural fibers; do not use it on acetate. It also removes hard-water scale from kettles and chrome fixtures. Full-strength vinegar is excellent for cleaning glass or taking rust off sinks and dishes. One gallon of hot water and $\frac{1}{4}$ cup of vinegar is a good all-purpose cleaner for appliances and vinyl or tile floors.

Baking soda—sodium bicarbonate—is a mild base that deodorizes, cuts grease, and provides gentle abrasion. Use it to scrub countertops, tile, ovens, and porcelain fixtures.

Vinegar and baking soda combine to create fizzing that can clear a partially clogged drain: Pour in $\frac{1}{4}$ cup baking soda, then $\frac{1}{2}$ cup vinegar, then close the drain. When the fizzing stops, flush the drain with boiling water.

HANDLING CHEMICALS WISELY

The labels of household cleaners provide signal words—followed by specific directions for use—that indicate the level of care with which to handle the product. "CAUTION" (or "WARNING") means that the product will irritate the skin or eyes, is harmful when ingested, or is somewhat flammable. "DANGER" indicates that the agent may harm skin or cause adverse effects if swallowed. "POISON," the strictest warning, signifies a chemical that can cause serious harm or even death if it contacts the skin or is taken internally. When using a cleaner labeled with any of these signal words, follow the written instructions, and keep the product out of the reach of children and pets.

Use only as much of a cleaning agent as you need to do the job and, unless specifically directed to do so, never mix different cleaners. Some combinations—such as ammonia and chlorine bleach—form compounds that emit fatal fumes. Leave products in their original containers, properly closed, and do not reuse the containers for other purposes.

Avoid splashing the product, and wear safety goggles, long sleeves, and gloves. Rubber kitchen gloves are adequate for some substances, but for harsh chemicals you'll need a special pair made of heavy-duty nitrile. When using a product that gives off noxious fumes, work outside or in a well-ventilated area and take frequent fresh-air breaks. If necessary, wear a respirator with cartridges appropriate for the chemical you are using.

When working with a flammable product, do not smoke; and keep away from heat, sparks, or flames. Extinguish pilot lights when working near a gas stove, clothes dryer, or water heater. Do not place anything that has been cleaned with a flammable agent into a clothes dryer.

If someone accidentally ingests a dangerous chemical, call an emergency room or poison prevention line immediately. Follow the instructions on the product label, which may direct that the person drink a glass of milk or water; do not induce vomiting unless advised to do so.

An Arsenal of Cleaning Tools

As with any task, cleaning is easier when you have the proper tools. For major jobs—such as buffing floors or scouring heavily soiled masonry —you may need to rent specialized equipment; but for most tasks, a basic set of implements is all you'll need *(below and page 12)*. To obtain top-quality tools, consider a trip to a janitorial supply store.

Besides these items, keep on hand a few other implements. A flexible-blade putty knife is ideal for scraping candle wax and chewing gum from hard surfaces. For mixing cleaning compounds, choose a polyethylene pail rather than a metal one, which can be damaged by acids and chlorine. The most effective dusters are made of lamb's wool or ostrich feathers, rather than chicken feathers or synthetics. Special dusting cloths with a tacky finish or a static charge or treated paper sheets also work well.

You'll also need cloth: Plain white cotton is preferable to synthetics for cleaning because it is absorbent; especially useful are terry-cloth toweling and cotton-knit fabrics such as old T-shirts.

Sandpaper and steel wool are essential for removing stubborn stains and for polishing surfaces. Stock several grades, from 20- to 600-grit in sandpaper and from #1 to #4/0 in steel wool.

DUSTPAN

NYLON BROOM

DUST MOP

Basic sweeping tools.

The best brooms have nylon bristles that won't break off and scatter. Bristles cut at an angle *(far left)* will get into tight corners more easily than the square-cut type.

Select a dustpan with a rubber lip to keep dirt from being swept underneath. A ridge along the edge prevents debris from spilling out. Pans with long handles save you the trouble of bending down.

A dust mop with a swiveling head is even more effective than a broom for picking up dust.

The right mop for the job.

The most effective mop for a given situation depends on the job. For large expanses of uncarpeted floor, a good choice is a string mop with a commercial-style wringer bucket. A sponge mop is more convenient for small kitchens and bathrooms, and does not require a wringer bucket.

WRINGER BUCKET

STRING MOP

SPONGE MOP

Scrubbing implements.

For general scouring, choose a nylon pad. These are often attached to a small handle, the back of a sponge, or a long extension handle. With many brands, the color of the pad indicates its level of abrasiveness: a black or brown pad is highly abrasive, white nonabrasive, and blue and green medium. Scrub most surfaces with the nonabrasive white pad.

For irregular surfaces, a scrub brush works better than a pad. Nylon bristles are more durable than natural bristles and dry more quickly. But natural bristles are required with acid, which will cause nylon to deteriorate. The length and diameter of the bristles determine their stiffness or softness. Scrub brushes are available in a number of sizes; some have threaded sockets for attaching long handles. Toothbrushes and shoe-polish applicators are ideal for getting into crannies such as those in wickerwork.

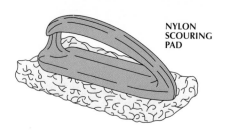

NYLON SCOURING PAD

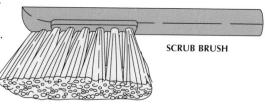
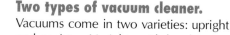

SCRUB BRUSH

UPRIGHT VACUUM

CANISTER VACUUM

Two types of vacuum cleaner.

Vacuums come in two varieties: upright and canister. Uprights with brushes on a rotating shaft called a beater bar are best suited for deep-cleaning carpets. With more suction than most uprights and with special hose attachments, canister vacuums excel at cleaning upholstery and uncarpeted floors, getting into crevices, and reaching areas above floor level. Hybrids—uprights with hose attachments and canister vacuums with a beater-bar nozzle—are also available. For convenience, buy an upright vacuum for carpets and a small canister for other jobs.

For vacuuming drapes and other lightweight objects, a suction-reducing feature is handy. If you have large surfaces to clean, you may want an upright model that moves forward automatically. Other convenient features are a retractable cord and an easy-to-change bag.

Reviving Wood Finishes

Most wood surfaces are protected by some sort of coating, ranging from clear varnishes on fine paneling to paints that mask the utilitarian woods of interior trim and exterior siding. Methods for cleaning them depend on the type of finish.

Paint: Exterior painted surfaces can be scrubbed down by hand *(page 15)*, or by a power washer *(pages 26-28)*. Interior surfaces can be washed with an all-purpose household detergent; wring out the cloth or sponge until it is almost dry.

Clear Finishes: Maintain clear finishes on furniture and paneling—including varnish, lacquer, shellac, and oil—by routine polishing and quick cleaning of spills. More rigorous methods are required to restore a faded or discolored finish; spots and blemishes need special treatment *(page 14)*. When the blemish extends to the wood itself, the only solution is to strip the wood and refinish it.

Often covered with wax for extra protection, varnish, lacquer, and shellac can be cleaned with a commercial cleaner/polish, usually sprayed on, then lightly rubbed with a soft, lint-free cloth. Use these products sparingly as they can build up over time.

An oil finish is best cleaned with a cloth dampened in boiled linseed oil. Pour a small amount of oil into the center of the cloth, then twist the cloth to distribute the oil.

Restore a clouded finish by rubbing it with a compatible substance, working in the direction of the grain and taking care not to rub through the finish.

For a faded oil finish, combine equal parts of turpentine and boiled linseed oil, then rub the mixture over the entire surface and wipe it away immediately. Allow the wood to stand for two or three days until it is dry, then repeat the process. Store the oiled cloth in a tightly sealed jar to eliminate the risk of spontaneous combustion.

Treat faded varnish, shellac, and lacquer finishes with a cloth dampened in lemon oil. Wipe the surface, moistening the cloth as necessary, until the cloudiness disappears. If the finish is dull after cleaning, apply a coat of paste wax and buff it.

Unfinished Wood: Unfinished exterior siding can be scrubbed and rinsed like painted surfaces *(page 15)*. For unfinished interior wood, use a dry sponge *(page 42)*.

Unfinished butcher block in the kitchen is a special case, because it is exposed regularly to water and food. Rub the surface with vegetable oil to seal the wood pores, wipe the wood clean after each use with a damp cloth, and reapply oil occasionally.

TOOLS

Cotton cloths
Sponges
Dry sponge
Cotton-tipped swab
Steel wool (#3/0)
Plastic pail
Long-handled
   stiff-bristle brush
Garden hose

Identifying a finish.
To determine the type of finish on a piece of furniture, begin by rubbing an inconspicuous spot with a cotton-tipped swab dipped in denatured alcohol *(right)*; a shellac finish will soften when moistened with alcohol. If the finish remains unaffected, dip a second swab in lacquer thinner and rub it over the surface; a lacquer finish will soften and then dry almost immediately. When neither test dissolves the finish, rub a mixture of turpentine and boiled linseed oil vigorously over a small area; if the mixture can be rubbed into the wood, the finish is oil—if not, it is varnish.

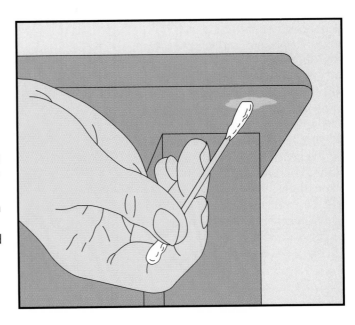

REMOVING SPOTS FROM WOODWORK

Blemish	Treatment					
	Damp cloth	Heavy-duty degreaser	Mineral spirits	#3/0 steel wool	Rottenstone/ mineral oil	3/F pumice/ mineral oil
Alcohol spots	1			2	3	4
Built-up wax			1			
Grease		1	2			
Ink	1			2	3	4
Oil-base paint			1	2	3	4
Water-base paint	1		2	3	4	5
Water spots			1	2	3	4
White rings or spots	1			2	3	4

Lifting blemishes from finished wood. Remedies for common problems with wood finishes are provided from left to right in order of increasing strength. Try the weakest cleaner first, proceeding to the next one only if necessary. If the finish is dulled by the treatment, revive it *(page 13)*.

Apply a degreaser with a cloth, then wipe the surface clean with a wet cloth and dry it well. To lift a spot from a wood surface with mineral spirits, dip a clean cloth into the solvent and rub it over the spot; change to a fresh cloth when the old one becomes discolored. If you're using steel wool, rub the spot lightly, making short back-and-forth passes; always work in the direction of the grain. Remove tough stains with rottenstone or pumice and mineral oil *(below)*.

Removing stubborn stains.
◆ Mix rottenstone and mineral oil into a creamy paste.
◆ With a clean cloth *(right)* or #3/0 steel wool, work the paste into the spot using back-and-forth motions, taking care not to rub through the finish.
◆ When the spot has disappeared, wipe off the paste with a cloth dampened with water, then dry the surface with a soft cloth.
◆ If the spot remains, apply 3/F pumice and mineral oil in the same manner.

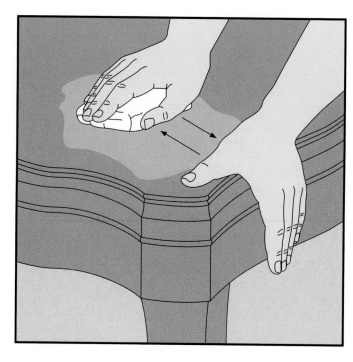

SCRUBBING DOWN WOOD SIDING

1. Applying the cleaner.
◆ Brush coarse dirt off the siding with a wadded cotton cloth.
◆ In a plastic pail, mix 1 gallon of water and $\frac{1}{4}$ cup automatic dishwasher detergent. For unfinished cedar siding, use a commercial cleaner designed specifically for cedar.
◆ Wearing goggles and rubber gloves, use a long-handled, stiff-bristle brush to scrub the siding with long lateral strokes *(right)*. Work in 5-foot-wide strips from the bottom up; this will prevent dirty water from soaking into dry siding below.

To get rid of mildew, first rinse the wall, then mix a solution of 1 quart of chlorine bleach and 1 gallon of water. Test it first by applying some in a hidden spot, then scrub the wall with it.

2. Rinsing away the dirt.
◆ Working from the top down, hose off the washed strip with a strong spray of clear water to remove the loosened dirt and the cleaning solution *(left)*.
◆ Continue washing and rinsing strips of siding, always washing from bottom to top and rinsing from top to bottom. With each rinse, flush off the adjacent wall surfaces to prevent the loosened dirt from resettling on another part of the wall.

For a high-pressure rinse, attach a pressure wand *(photograph)* to the end of your garden hose. This model has a canister to dispense the cleaning agent as well.

The finish on a wood floor protects it from wear and seals it against dust and spilled liquids. Before cleaning a floor, determine the type of finish on it *(below)*. Older floors often have penetrating finishes. These soak into the wood pores and require waxing. Modern flooring more often has a surface finish—typically polyurethane—which forms a protective film and does not need to be waxed.

Waxed Penetrating Finishes: To prolong the life of the wax, vacuum or dust-mop the floor weekly before dirt and dust are pressed into the surface. Wipe up spills immediately with a dry cloth or paper towel; use a barely damp cloth for sticky spills. Blemishes can be lifted with the products described on page 113. When the wax loses its luster, it can sometimes be restored by buffing *(page 18)*. If this fails, you can apply more wax, but after two or three coats, the old wax should be stripped first *(opposite)*. For stripping, use a cleaning/renovating product designed for wood floors; it will both clean and reseal the wood. Before

rewaxing, vacuum the floor thoroughly; otherwise, any surface dirt will be incorporated into the new wax.

If the wax is worn through in one spot, treat that area only. If the damage extends to the wood itself, the spot can be repaired as described opposite.

Buffing waxes are available in two forms: paste and liquid. Both varieties have a solvent base and differ only in the amount of solvent they contain. The thicker paste waxes tend to be more durable and are a good choice for old floors because they fill in small cracks. But liquid buffing waxes are easier to apply, and are adequate for most floors.

Surface Finishes: Vacuum or dust-mop these floors regularly and wipe up spills immediately. Worn spots in the finish can sometimes be patched *(opposite)*, but often the area will not blend in well with the rest of the floor. If you are not satisfied with the results, try refinishing the entire floorboard end to end.

If the floor was waxed, care for it as you would one with a penetrating finish.

TOOLS

Vacuum
Dust mop
Cotton cloths
Steel wool (#1, #3/0)
Paintbrush
Floor buffer
Steel-wool pad for buffer
Soft-bristle polishing
   pad for buffer
White nylon pad
   for buffer
Fleece wax applicator

Identifying the finish.
Check whether the floor is waxed by scraping a low-traffic spot with a fingernail; if you can scrape off material, it is waxed. If not, scratch an inconspicuous spot with a coin *(right)*. The coin will make a powdery white mark on a surface finish; if it makes no mark, the finish is the penetrating type.

REFINISHING A SMALL AREA

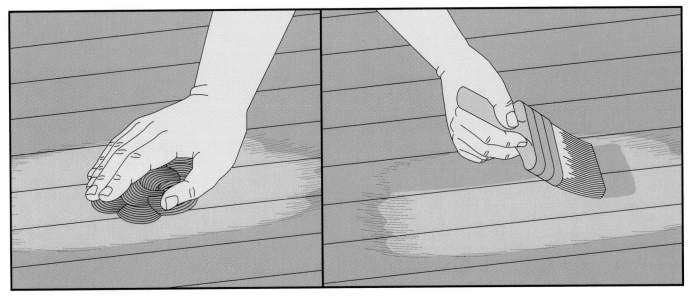

Treating the spot.
◆ Remove any wax from the worn area using a cloth moistened with mineral spirits.
◆ With #1 steel wool, rub down to the bare wood, working from the center outward *(above, left)*. (If you plan to apply a water-base finish, use 120-grit sandpaper.) Polish the edges of the spot to feather them into the surrounding finish.
◆ Sweep or vacuum up the dust. If the color of the wood does not match the rest of the floor, apply a matching stain and let it dry.
◆ With a 3-inch paintbrush, apply a very thin layer of finish over the bare spot, working with the wood grain in smooth, even strokes to avoid air bubbles *(above, right)*. Feather the new finish into the old by starting at the center and lifting the brush at the edge of the spot.
◆ Let the new finish dry, then apply additional coats in the same manner.
◆ If the floor was waxed originally, rewax the spot and buff it with a soft cloth.

STRIPPING AND REWAXING A FLOOR

1. Removing the old wax.
◆ Open all doors and windows to provide ventilation.
◆ Pour a commercial cleaner/renovator over a 2-foot-square area.
◆ Rub the chemical into the floor with a rented floor buffer equipped with a steel-wool pad.
◆ As the wax dissolves, put on rubber gloves and wipe it up immediately with a lint-free absorbent cloth *(left)*.
◆ Continue cleaning small sections—changing or turning the pad over when it becomes clogged—until you have covered the entire floor.
◆ Remove residual wax by letting the floor dry and rubbing it lightly with a dry pad of #3/0 steel wool.
◆ Sweep or vacuum up any remaining wax powder.

2. Applying new wax.

◆ If you're applying liquid wax, pour a saucer-sized pool of it on the floor near one wall and spread it with a fleece wax applicator *(inset)*.

◆ Let the wax dry for about 30 minutes, then attach a soft-bristle polishing brush to the floor buffer. Working on one small section at a time, guide the buffer from side to side, paralleling the floorboards *(right)*. To change direction, tilt the machine slightly forward or backward.

◆ Buff the edges of the floor with a soft cloth.

◆ Install a white nylon pad on the buffer and go over the floor once to brighten the shine and eliminate any swirl marks.

If you're using paste wax, wrap a lump of wax in a cotton cloth (a sock works well). Rub the cloth on the floor to apply a thin layer—the warmth of your hand will soften the wax. Buff the floor in the same way you would for liquid wax.

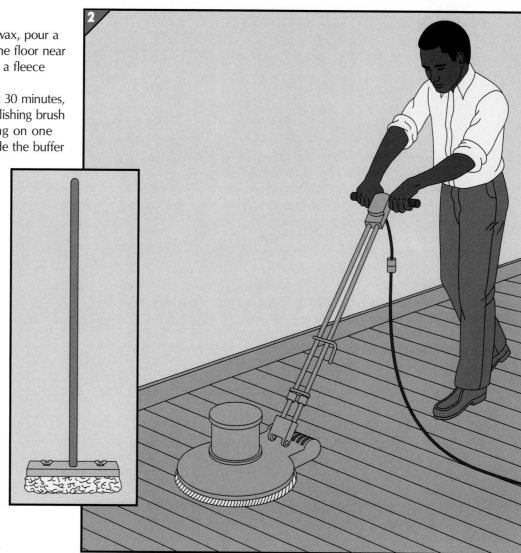

A LIGHTWEIGHT HOME BUFFER

For buffing waxed floors or adding wax without removing the existing layer, consider buying a lightweight buffer *(left)* rather than renting a heavy-duty model. The buffer weighs only 24 pounds—light enough to be operated with one hand and hung on a wall for storage. It can be equipped with a polishing pad or a fleece pad to buff floors to a high gloss.

Most woven furniture is made from one or more of five types of fibers *(right)*, each requiring a different method of cleaning. Scrub rattan with a soft-bristle brush dipped in warm, soapy water. Mist unfinished rattan once a year with a garden hose to keep it from drying out and becoming brittle. Do not hose rattan that has been painted or coated with a clear finish, rattan used in combination with fibers other than cane, or wood furniture accented with rattan; rather, moisten the rattan component of the furniture with a damp cloth. Mist cane with water, and clean it as you would rattan, taking care not to mar the finish on any surrounding wood. Since reed is highly absorbent, wash it with as little water as possible—a damp cloth will usually do—and avoid hosing or misting it. Individual strands of fiber rush will unravel when soaked; clean it only with a damp cloth and never spray it with water. Like fiber rush, sea grass tends to unravel when it is saturated. Wipe it clean with a damp cloth, and do not spray it with water.

TOOLS

Soft-bristle brush
Cotton cloths
House-plant mister

Wicker Materials.
The structural framework of wicker furniture is usually made up of rattan stalks in their natural form. Seats and chair backs are commonly woven from cane, the glossy covering that sheathes the rattan stalk. Reed—the smooth core of the rattan plant—is widely used for the woven covering of wicker furniture. Made of kraft paper fashioned to resemble natural rush, fiber rush is woven into chair seats. Twisted strands of sea grass—also known as Hong Kong grass—are used for weaving chair seats.

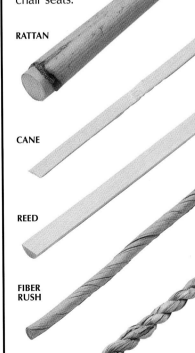

RATTAN

CANE

REED

FIBER RUSH

SEA GRASS

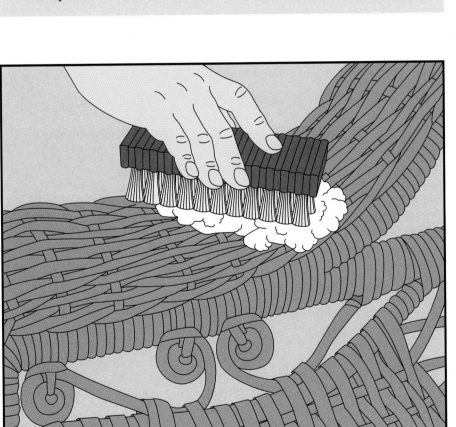

Deep-cleaning wicker.
◆ Wipe off surface dirt with a damp cloth.
◆ Dip a small brush in warm, soapy water and shake it vigorously to throw off most of the water.
◆ Scrub interior parts and intricate scrollwork with short, straight strokes, following the weave direction *(above)*.
◆ Rinse the piece by dipping the brush in clear water and again shaking it almost dry, then scrubbing out the residual soap.

Removing Grime from Masonry

To clean masonry—whatever the surface—start with elbow grease rather than strong chemicals. Use them as a last resort, particularly on decorative masonry like marble and slate. Cleaning these surfaces calls for patience, especially in the final stages, when some effort is needed to erase any lingering shadow of a spot or stain.

Routine Cleaning: The power of a scrub brush and an all-purpose detergent should not be overlooked. Many spots and stains will yield to such treatment. If not, try a heavy-duty degreaser or scouring powder. Be warned, however, that stronger cleaners may dull the polished surface of stone, which will later have to be restored.

Getting Tough on Grime: Some stains and blemishes require more abrasion than a scrub brush can supply, such as brick speckled with paint or discolored by ivy *(below)*. Efflorescence—a white powdery deposit on brick—and oil and grease spills or hardened lumps of plastic-base products on concrete need special treatment *(opposite)*.

For large outdoor masonry surfaces, such as the brick wall of a house or a concrete driveway, you can rent a pressure washer *(pages 26-28)*. This device delivers a stream of water at pressures sufficient to blast out all but the most deeply ingrained dirt. For embedded stains that have worked into the pores of masonry surfaces, draw them out with a poultice *(page 22)*.

Restoring the Appearance: Once the dirt or stain has been removed, you may have to take measures to erase the effects of your cleaning. Concrete and brick surfaces generally require nothing more than a thorough rinsing; marble and slate, on the other hand, may need buffing *(page 23)*.

Protecting the Surface: Although sealing brick is not recommended, you can protect clean concrete or stone against soil by applying a commercial concrete sealer, which is available at paint and hardware stores; however, this product will impart a slightly unnatural gloss to the surface. Sealing asphalt fills hairline cracks and restores the surface color *(page 25)*.

 TOOLS

Stiff-bristle brush (natural-bristle for acid)
Pressure washer
Plastic pail
Dustpan
Propane torch
Putty knife
Electric drill with buffing attachment
Sanding block
Wet-or-dry sandpaper (600-grit)
Paint roller
Pressurized garden sprayer
Sponge applicator
Combination brush-and-squeegee

 SAFETY TIPS

Put on goggles when sanding or using a propane torch.

DISLODGING SURFACE DEPOSITS

Sanding stains off brick.
◆ Break a matching brick into fragments and choose a piece that will comfortably fit your hand.
◆ Working slowly and pressing lightly, rub the broken surface of the fragment over the deposits with a back-and-forth motion *(right)*. Use only the broken surface of the brick—the smooth faces could scratch the brickwork.

Dissolving efflorescence.

◆ Working on one small section at a time, scrub the wall with a dry scrub brush *(left)*.

◆ If brushing doesn't work, buy an acid-base cleaning product designed for brick. Protect the ground under the wall and nearby plants with plastic sheeting. Wearing rubber rain gear, nitrile gloves, rubber boots, goggles, and a face shield, add 1 part of the cleaner to 10 parts water in a plastic pail. Test it on an inconspicuous area.

◆ Soak the masonry with plain water.

◆ Using a natural-bristle scrub brush, scrub the wall with the mixture.

◆ Let the product sit for 10 minutes, then rinse it off with a garden hose.

! **CAUTION** *Always pour an acid-base product into water—never add water to an acid. When working indoors, open all windows and keep the air moving with fans. If your nose or eyes begin to sting, leave the room immediately and splash your face with cold water. Do not continue using the cleaner until the stinging subsides.*

Soaking up grease and oil.

◆ Flood the surface with mineral spirits to dissolve heavy deposits.

◆ Cover the stain with clay-base cat litter or fuller's earth and let it stand for several hours until it has soaked up the grease or oil; then sweep it up *(left)*.

◆ Wearing rubber gloves, scrub away any residual stain with a heavy-duty degreaser.

◆ If oil or grease has soaked below the surface, apply a poultice *(page 22)*.

Burning plastic off concrete.

◆ Holding a propane torch about 6 inches above the surface, play the flame slowly back and forth on the hardened plastic *(left)*; it will begin to give off an acrid black smoke. Avoid keeping the flame on one spot too long—it can damage the concrete.

◆ When the plastic is reduced to ashes, turn off the torch and sweep up the ashes.

! **CAUTION** *Remove all flammable objects from the area and keep a fire extinguisher handy. If you are working indoors, open at least two windows for cross ventilation and set a fan in one of the windows to speed the airflow.*

When substances penetrate deep into masonry, they may leave persistent stains that require the special treatment of a poultice. For the types of stains listed here, make poultices by mixing just enough of the recommended liquid cleaning agent with talc, whiting, or lime to make a thick paste. Spread a $\frac{1}{4}$-inch layer over the stain and cover it with plastic, sealing the edges with masking tape *(below)*. Leave the poultice in place until it dries, then scrape it off with a putty knife. Rinse the area well as recommended. Several treatments may be necessary before the stain is completely gone.

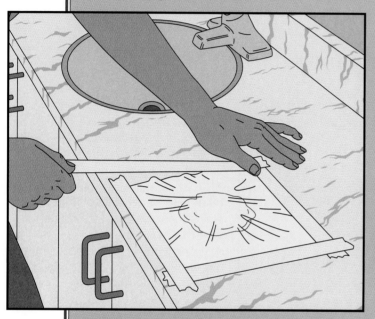

When preparing or applying poultices, wear goggles, a dust mask, and long sleeves as well as the type of gloves recommended for the agent, and keep the work area well ventilated.

Asphalt or Tar: Scrape off excess material with a putty knife, then scrub the spot with scouring powder and hot water. If the stain lingers, put on a pair of polyvinyl alcohol (PVA) gloves, and apply a poultice prepared with trichloroethylene obtained from a paint store. After removing the poultice, scrub the area again.

Blood: Wet the stain with water. Wearing nitrile gloves, cover the stain with a thin layer of sodium peroxide powder. Dampen the powder with a little water and let it stand for a few minutes. Add more water and scrub the area with a stiff-bristle brush. Pour vinegar on the spot to neutralize any alkaline residue, then rinse it with water.

Caulk or Chewing Gum: Scrape off as much of the material as possible. Wearing rubber gloves, apply a poultice prepared with isopropyl alcohol. After the poultice is dry, brush it away and wash the surface with a heavy-duty degreaser.

Coffee or Tea: Put on rubber gloves to make a poultice of 1 part glycerin, 2 parts isopropyl alcohol, and 4 parts water. Apply it to the stain. Repeat the application up to three times if necessary. If the blemish is still visible after the third treatment, switch to a poultice prepared with chlorine bleach diluted to one-quarter strength.

Grease: Wearing rubber gloves, scrub the spot with a heavy-duty degreaser, then apply a poultice made with an oil-dissolving solvent, available at an auto-supply store. Or, wearing PVA gloves, treat the area with trichloroethylene.

Ink: Some inks can be removed from masonry by scrubbing with scouring powder; but the ink from a felt-tipped pen responds only to types of bleach. You may need to experiment to determine which compound works best. Wearing rubber gloves, try a poultice made with diluted chlorine bleach or bleaching powder. Put on nitrile gloves to apply calcium hypochlorite, available at swimming-pool-supply stores; a mildew remover; or a poultice made with household ammonia.

Nonferrous Metals: To remove the blue or green stains left by copper, brass, or bronze, put on nitrile gloves and make a poultice with sal ammoniac and household ammonia. For the white powdery stains left by corroding aluminum, use the same treatment as for efflorescence *(page 21)*.

Paint: Blot fresh paint spills with rags or paper towels; work gently without wiping, which could spread the paint and embed it in the surface. After the excess paint has been blotted up, scrub out the remainder: For latex-base paint, use scouring powder and water; for oil-base paints, wear nitrile gloves and apply mineral spirits. To remove dried paint, start with a poultice prepared with commercial paint remover. Put on nitrile gloves and scrub the remaining stain with steel wool or a scouring powder.

Tobacco: Apply a poultice of scouring powder and hot water; when the mixture dries, scrape it off and rinse the area with hot water.

Polishing with jeweler's rouge.

◆ Install a cloth-covered buffing attachment on an electric drill.
◆ Press a bar of jeweler's rouge or stone-polishing compound against the edge of the revolving wheel hard enough to charge the wheel liberally with pol-

ish *(above, left)*, but not so hard as to mat the fibers.
◆ Touch the buffing wheel lightly against the stone and work it slowly back and forth until the surface is smooth *(above, right)*.
◆ Wash the polished surface with hot, soapy water to remove any residual compound.

Sanding out scratches.

◆ Wrap a sanding block with ultrafine (600-grit) wet-or-dry sandpaper, moistened with water.
◆ Pressing the sanding block against the scratched area, rub hard in circular strokes until the surface is smooth.
◆ Restore the gloss by sprinkling powdered tin oxide—available from lapidary-supply stores—onto the surface. Add just enough water to make a thick paste. Flip the sandpaper smooth side out and wrap it over the sanding block; resume rubbing until the stone is glossy *(right)*.
◆ Wash the surface with warm, soapy water, then rinse it clean.
◆ Polish the stone with jeweler's rouge *(above)*.

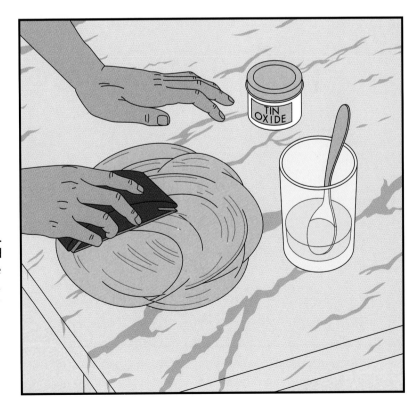

APPLYING A PROTECTIVE SEALER

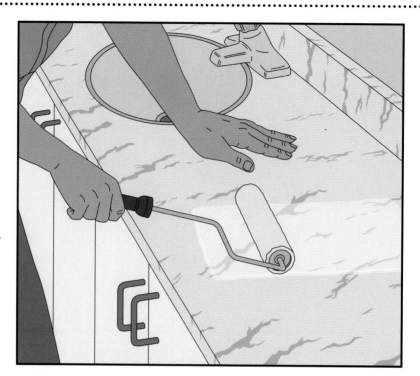

Sealing stone.

◆ Using a paint roller with a short nap—a $\frac{1}{4}$-inch nap works best—apply a thin film of silicone sealer to the surface *(right)*. Along the edges, use a cloth pad saturated with sealer.

◆ Allow the stone to dry for 45 to 60 minutes, then apply a second coat.

Protecting concrete.

◆ For outdoor jobs, fill a pressurized garden sprayer with a concrete sealer and work the pump up and down several times to pressurize the tank.

◆ Wearing goggles, lightly fog the entire surface, holding the sprayer nozzle 12 to 18 inches away *(above)*.

◆ Go over the area again, working the sprayer back and forth until the concrete is flooded with as much sealer as it can absorb.

On indoor surfaces, spread the sealer with a sponge applicator.

COATING AN ASPHALT DRIVEWAY

1. Applying the emulsion.

◆ Clean the surface with a hose; wearing rubber gloves, remove any oil or grease with a heavy-duty degreaser.

◆ Fill any holes and cracks wider than $\frac{1}{8}$ inch with asphalt-patching compound.

◆ If the surface has dried, dampen it lightly.

◆ Beginning along one edge of the driveway, pour a thick ribbon of coal-tar pitch emulsion 3 feet long onto the surface *(right)*—one 5-gallon pail of emulsion will coat about 400 square feet. For a nonslip surface, buy a product containing sand.

2. Spreading the sealer.

◆ With the squeegee side of a combination brush-and-squeegee tool *(photograph)*, spread the emulsion all the way across the surface in a 3-foot-wide swath.

◆ Turn the tool to the brush side and smooth out the coating with the bristles.

◆ Apply and spread more emulsion, coating the surface in 3-foot sections *(above)*, until the entire driveway is covered.

◆ Keep traffic off the drive for 24 hours.

Blasting Off Dirt with Water

Power washers—available at tool-rental agencies—can dramatically speed the cleaning of exterior walls, driveways, patios, and sidewalks. A powerful pump in the unit draws water from a faucet and blasts it at high pressure through a nozzle. The spray loosens and washes away dirt and grime.

Choosing Equipment: While gas-powered washers can deliver water at greater pressure and volume, electric models are easier to use and are adequate for most small jobs. Each machine has a low-pressure nozzle

for applying detergent and a selection of high-pressure nozzles for washing. The high-pressure nozzles disperse water in a wide or narrow stream; for most purposes, use one that delivers a 25-degree spray.

Operating the Washer: Plain water is often used to blast away dirt, but you can add a detergent to boost the cleaning power. Choose a product designed for use with the washer, and adjust the dilution on the machine according to the instructions on the label. The pressure of the spray is regulated by a control

on the machine or on the nozzle; however, have the rental agency set the pressure—typically 1500 pounds per square inch (psi) for wood and vinyl, and no more than 700 psi for brick.

 Never point the nozzle **CAUTION** *at anyone—the high-pressure jet of water can cause severe injury. Before leaving the washer unattended, shut off the motor and squeeze the trigger to relieve the pressure. Never use a gas-powered unit indoors.*

 TOOLS

Pressure washer
Garden hose

🪖 **SAFETY TIPS**

Protect your eyes with goggles when operating a pressure washer.

Setting up a power washer.

Not all power washers are configured like the one at right; ask the rental agency for a demonstration of how to hook up the hoses for your model. Usually a $\frac{3}{4}$-inch garden hose connects the machine to an exterior faucet, and another hose, furnished with the unit, links the cleaning-solution container to the pump. A third hose, also provided, joins the spray wand and the unit. A mixing valve adjusts the dilution of the cleaning agent.

For safety, plug the washer into an outlet protected by a ground-fault circuit interrupter (GFCI), or use an extension cord with a GFCI to connect it to an unprotected outlet. Shield the receptacle by taping plastic over it.

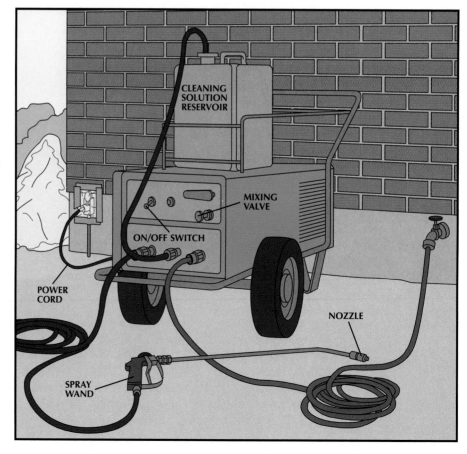

1. Preparing the house.
◆ Seal exterior electrical outlets and soffit vents with overlapping strips of plastic tape.
◆ Close all doors and windows.
◆ Protect nearby plants by draping them with large plastic bags or drop cloths.
◆ Tie heavyweight plastic bags around outdoor light fixtures to protect them from water damage *(left)*.
◆ Water the earth around the wall thoroughly to dilute any cleaning chemicals that seep into the soil.

2. Venting the lines.
◆ Put on goggles and gloves and, to keep dry, a hooded rain jacket and pants, and rubber boots.
◆ Connect the hoses *(opposite)* and turn the faucet on all the way.
◆ Without turning the motor on, point the spray wand toward the ground and squeeze the trigger to vent air from the lines.
◆ When a steady stream of water flows through the wand *(right)*, release the trigger and snap the low-pressure spray nozzle onto the wand.

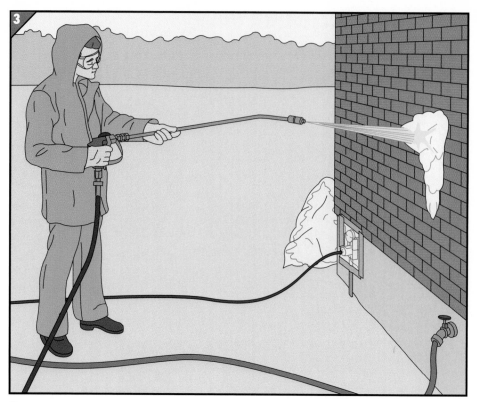

3. Applying the chemical.

◆ Fill the cleaning-solution reservoir and open the mixing valve.

◆ Turn on the motor; then, holding the wand about 2 feet from the wall, squeeze the trigger, and working from the bottom to the top of a section, move the wand back and forth in 6- to 8-foot strokes *(above)*.

◆ Turn off the unit and the mixing valve. Point the wand in a safe direction and pull the trigger to release the pressure.

4. Driving off the dirt.

◆ Install a high-pressure nozzle with a 25-degree spray and vent the lines *(page 27, Step 2)*. Then turn the unit back on.

◆ Grasp the spray wand firmly before squeezing the trigger so the recoil does not jerk the equipment out of your hands. Holding the wand about 1 foot away from a brick wall or 2 feet from wood or vinyl, aim at an inconspicuous spot and press the trigger. Quickly step away from the wall if there is any sign of damage to the surface; hold the wand further away and try again.

◆ Starting at the top and working down, move the wand across successive sections of the wall in gentle side-to-side sweeps *(right)*.

Without the protection of paint, oil, or lacquer, many metals become rusted or tarnished by oxygen and airborne salts and acids. The method for cleaning depends on the type of metal and on whether it is protected with a finish *(pages 114-115)*.

Decorative Metals: Smudges and light tarnish can usually be removed from silver, brass, copper, and pewter with a commercial metal cleaner *(page 30)*. The best polishes are those formulated for a particular metal; some silver polishes contain chemicals that retard tarnishing. Since metal polishes generally include a fine abrasive that actually rubs away some of the metal, don't polish any more often than necessary. Nonabrasive cleaners, designed to bathe objects, are available for silver. These products clean but they do not polish.

For heavy tarnish on brass exposed to the weather, use a special stripping solution *(below)*. After polishing the item, coat it with a clear protective finish such as polymerized tung oil *(page 30)*. Highly resistant to water, alcohol, acids, and heat, it can be buffed to a lustrous finish that does not darken over time as lacquers do. With age, paint and lacquer coatings on metal are prone to chipping, scratching, and peeling, and will have to be removed with strippers. These finishes cannot be rubbed with abrasives or cleaned with the harsh chemicals used to remove tarnish.

Steel, Aluminum, and Iron: Metal surfaces normally left uncoated—a stainless-steel sink or an aluminum door frame, for example—usually need only a thorough washing with mild liquid detergent and water. Rust on iron can be removed with steel wool, a wire brush, or a wire-brush drill attachment *(page 32)*.

To clean stubborn dirt, paint, or rust from large areas of metal outdoors—a chain-link or wrought-iron fence, for example—rent a sandblaster *(page 32)*. Primer and paint can then be applied to some objects to prevent a recurrence. Aluminum siding can be cleaned in the same way as wood siding *(page 15)*.

Metal Blinds: Louvered window shades, particularly horizontal ones, collect dirt easily. Dust them every month or so, and clean them occasionally *(page 31)*.

TOOLS

Steel wool	Soft-bristle scrub brush	Electric drill with wire-brush attachment
Wire brush	Shoe brush	
Pail	Cotton cloths	Sandblaster

SAFETY TIPS

Wear goggles when working with an electric drill with a wire-brush attachment.

When sandblasting, put on a rain suit, work gloves, a dust mask, and a face shield.

BRINGING BACK THE GLEAM OF BRASS

1. Soaking off heavy tarnish.

◆ In a glass container, prepare a stripping solution of 1 quart water, 1 cup vinegar, and $\frac{1}{4}$ cup salt.

◆ Soak the brass object in the solution overnight. If the item cannot be immersed, wrap it in a clean cloth saturated with solution and enclose the wrapping in plastic *(right)*, tying the entire package with string.

◆ The next day, take the object out of the solution or remove the wrappings. Apply brass cleaner with a damp cloth; then rinse the item with water and a clean cloth.

2. Sealing brass with tung oil.

◆ Wearing nitrile gloves, remove old lacquer with a clean cloth dipped in lacquer thinner.

◆ Polish the object with a soft cloth, then warm it in the sun or place it in a 150°F oven for about 20 minutes.

◆ Immerse the warmed brass in a container of tung oil, suspending it from a string wrapped around a dowel *(left)*. Support the dowel between two pieces of scrap wood.

◆ Keep the object in the container for about 2 minutes so the oil seeps into all the crevices.

◆ Remove it from the oil and, with the object still suspended, air-dry it for about 15 minutes, letting the oil set.

◆ Buff off excess oil with a soft, lint-free cloth, taking care to avoid smudging the surface.

◆ Let the object dry for about 4 hours in a dust-free area.

For objects too large to be immersed, rub oil over the surface with a clean, lint-free cotton cloth.

⚠ **CAUTION** *Cloths soaked in solvents or refinishing products and then stored carelessly can ignite spontaneously; hang soaked cloths outdoors to dry, or store them in airtight metal or glass containers.*

POLISHING SILVER

Using silver polish.

◆ Pour some polish onto a clean lint-free cloth and coat the object thoroughly, rubbing gently *(right)*.

◆ Let the polish dry, then rub the object vigorously with a clean cloth until the polish has been removed and the shine is restored.

◆ Rinse and dry the metal.

TRICKS OF THE TRADE

Cleaning Silver with Chemistry

Plain, undecorated silver can be cleaned by a chemical process called electrolysis. Do not use the process on objects with satin or antique finishes or raised designs, or on flatware with hollow handles. Place a piece of aluminum foil in a container and set the silver object on the foil. Pour in 1 quart of boiling water mixed with $\frac{1}{4}$ teaspoon baking soda and $\frac{1}{4}$ teaspoon salt. After a few minutes, remove it from the solution and rinse it.

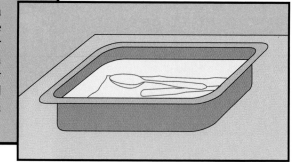

Cleaning horizontal blinds.
◆ Close the blind and turn the slats to the horizontal position. Dust the slats—for miniblinds, a special tool that fits between the slats works well *(photograph)*.
◆ Close the slats, then take the blind down. For a large blind, set it outdoors on a blanket on a flat surface. A small blind can be washed in a bathtub.

◆ Rinse the blind with water, then scrub one side with a soft-bristle brush and a solution of general-purpose detergent and warm water *(above)*.
Turn the blind over and clean the other side.
◆ With a helper holding the blind, or hanging it over a clothesline, rinse it thoroughly, then let it dry.

Wiping vertical blinds.
◆ Spread a plastic drop cloth on the floor under the blind; lay newspapers on the plastic to absorb water.
◆ Close the blind, turn the slats perpendicular to the window, and dust them.
◆ Dampen a soft cotton cloth in a solution of general-purpose detergent and warm water, and squeeze excess moisture from the cloth so the liquid won't drip into the tracks.
◆ Wipe both sides of each slat from top to bottom *(left)*.
◆ Rinse each slat with a damp cloth.

BRUSHING AWAY RUST AND DIRT

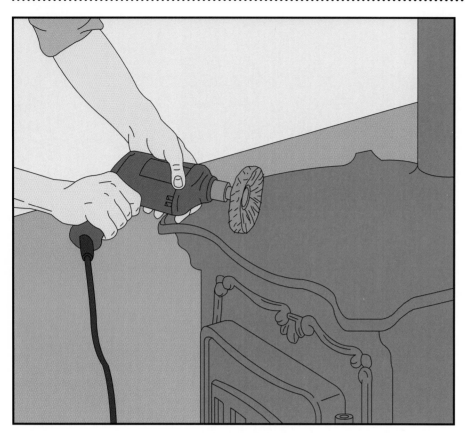

Wire-brushing the surface.
◆ Fit a wire-brush attachment on an electric drill and lightly abrade the metal surface until it is clean (left).
◆ If the metal surface is painted, touch up the paint.

For stoves coated with polish, apply more stove polish with a soft cloth. When the surface is dry, buff it with a shoe brush.

SANDBLASTING METALWORK

Removing dirt and rust.
◆ Place a drop cloth under the metalwork and over nearby shrubs and windows.
◆ Attach the air-line hose to the air compressor.
◆ Fill the sandblaster canister with silica sand of the appropriate grit for the model. Turn on the switch on the unit.
◆ Grasp the sandblaster firmly—one hand supporting the underside and the other on the handle-and-trigger assembly. Hold the nozzle 1 to 2 feet away from the metal and pull the trigger; direct the jet of sand up, down, and sideways over one area of the surface until it is clean (right).
◆ Refill the canister with fresh sand as necessary.

Plastics in the home are easy to clean, usually requiring little more than a sponging with mild detergent and warm water. For stubborn stains, try scrubbing with a paste of baking powder and water or a white nylon scouring pad. Avoid harsh cleaners and abrasives as they can damage plastic surfaces.

Acrylics: Found in clear form in storm windows, skylights, shower doors, and picture frames, this shatterproof plastic also comes in an opaque form for countertops. On clear acrylics, avoid cleaning fluids that contain alcohol, acetone, benzene, or carbon tetrachloride, which may soften or cloud the surface. Special cleaners designed for acrylic help prevent the surface from clouding. Scratches in acrylic can be sanded out *(pages 35-36)*.

Fiberglass: A light but exceptionally strong material, fiberglass is molded into a variety of shapes, including bathtubs, shower stalls, sinks, and patio roofing. Dull surfaces can often be restored with an automotive buffing compound.

Laminates: This plastic covering is found on countertops, tables, and cabinets. You may be able to disguise knife scratches with a coat of paste wax; deeper scratches can be filled with special patching compounds *(page 36)*.

Vinyls: A versatile family of plastics, vinyl turns up in floor coverings, the flexible webbing of garden furniture, and soft fabrics like shower curtains and artificial leather upholstery.

Regular vinyl flooring can be protected with a coat of acrylic floor polish, also referred to as wax. When the polish builds up and yellows, strip the floor and recoat it *(below)*. Even "no-wax" vinyl floors need waxing once the glossy finish wears down. Vinyl shower curtains and tablecloths can be cleaned in warm water in a washing machine, using the gentle wash and rinse cycles. Remove the items from the machine before the spin cycle and hang them up to dry after shaking off excess water. Vinyl siding can be cleaned the same way as wood *(page 15)*, and vinyl blinds like aluminum ones *(page 31)*. Vinyl furniture can be sprayed with mild detergent *(page 61)*.

TOOLS

Sponge
Nylon scouring pad (white)
Vacuum
Sponge mop
Cotton cloths
Long-handled nylon
    scouring pad (black)
Squeegee
Dustpan
Fleece wax applicator
Sanding block
Wet-or-dry sandpaper
    (400-grit)
C-clamps
Electric drill, muslin and
    fleece buffing disks
Putty knife

RECOATING VINYL FLOORS

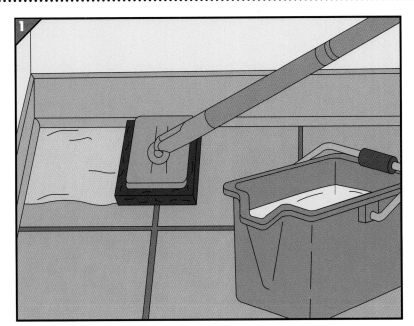

1. Softening the old polish.
◆ Vacuum the floor, then open the doors and windows to ensure good ventilation.
◆ Wearing rubber gloves, use a sponge mop to apply wax stripper formulated for vinyl floors.
◆ Let the stripper sit for the recommended time—usually about 10 minutes—then scrub the floor with a black or brown nylon scouring pad, preferably on a long handle *(left)*.
◆ Remove the polish immediately *(Step 2)*.

2. Removing the polish.

◆ With a squeegee and dustpan, scoop up the loosened polish *(left)*. If any polish remains stuck to the floor, scrub it again with the scouring pad.

◆ Rinse the floor immediately with a clean sponge mop.

3. Applying new polish.

◆ Vacuum the floor.

◆ Pour a small pool of polish onto the floor *(inset)* and apply it with a fleece wax applicator *(above)*. Spread the polish in slightly overlapping sweeps, adding more when it no longer spreads evenly.

◆ Let the wax dry for the recommended time—usually about 30 minutes—then apply a second coat to high-traffic areas.

POLISHING AN ACRYLIC STORM WINDOW

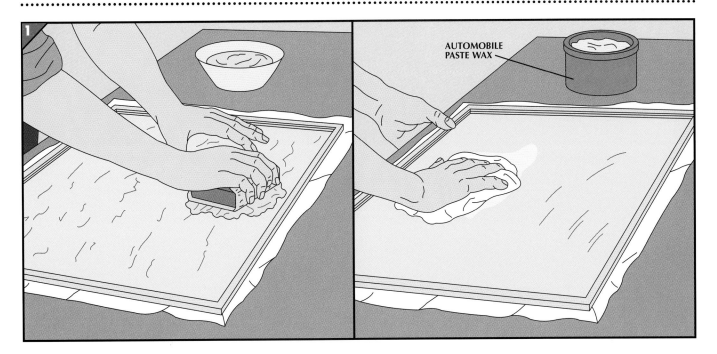

1. Sanding out the scratches.
Lay the window on a soft cloth. For deep scratches, fit a sanding block with 400-grit wet-or-dry sandpaper. Wet the paper and gently rub the block across the surface back and forth *(above, left)*, extending your strokes several inches beyond the scratches. Then restore the window's luster *(Step 2)*.

For shallow scratches, apply a thin, even coat of automobile paste wax, then buff the surface lightly with a soft cotton cloth *(above, right)*.

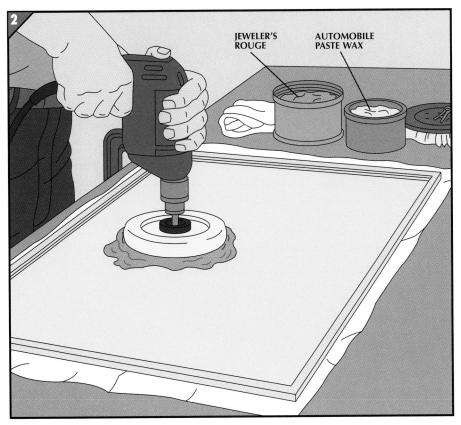

2. Restoring the luster.
◆ Clamp the window to the work surface.
◆ Fit an electric drill with a 4-inch buffing wheel covered with a muslin buffing disk. Apply jeweler's rouge to the disk and buff the entire pane in small, overlapping loops *(left)*.
◆ Once the sanding marks have disappeared, wash away the buffing compound with soap and water.
◆ Apply a coat of automobile paste wax to the surface with a clean fleece buffing disk.
◆ When the desired luster is achieved, wipe the surface with a clean, damp cloth to eliminate dust-attracting static charges.

Sanding out scratches in acrylic.
◆ Rub the scratched area with a sanding block covered with moistened 400-grit wet-or-dry sandpaper. Move the block in large circles—about the size of your hand—until the scratches disappear.
◆ Scrub the surface with a white nylon scouring pad and water *(left)*.

Filling scratches in laminates.
◆ On a plastic plate, squeeze a small quantity of plastic filler intended for laminate surfaces in a color matching your countertop. Work it with a clean putty knife until it begins to thicken.
◆ Wipe the scratch with a cloth moistened with the solvent supplied with the filler, then press the paste into the scratch with a putty knife *(right)*.
◆ Immediately wipe away excess material with the solvent-dampened cloth.
◆ If the filler shrinks as it hardens, wait an hour and repeat the process.

> ⚠ **CAUTION** *Hang the solvent-dampened cloth outside to dry or store it in an airtight metal or glass container.*

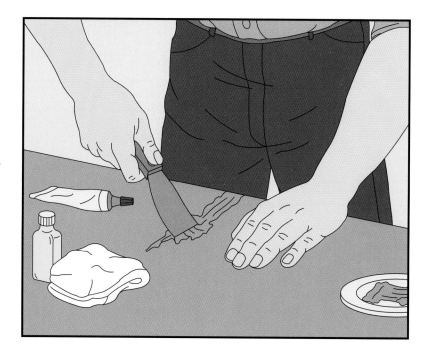

TRICKS OF THE TRADE

A Quick Fix for Light Scratches

Shallow scratches in countertops can be filled with a crayon. Select one in a matching color and rub it back and forth along the scratch until the depression is filled with wax; remove any excess with a soft cloth.

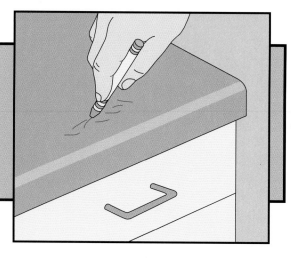

Cleaning Glass

Small glass surfaces, such as table-tops or mirrors, are easy to clean with spray-on window cleaner and a lint-free cloth. For a crystal chandelier, use special spray available at lamp-supply stores *(page 39)*. Washing the windows in an average house can be an all-day task. But with the right tool—a squeegee used by professional window washers—the job is not so difficult.

Washing Windows: A good-quality squeegee has two rubber blades with knife-sharp edges locked in a metal housing. You can buy a professional-quality squeegee at a janitorial supplier. These tools come in various sizes. For standard-size windows, choose one wide enough to cover 60 to 70 percent of the window in one vertical stroke, so only two strokes are needed to clean the surface *(page 38, top)*. Larger windows are cleaned in a continuous sideways motion without lifting the blade from the glass *(page 38, bottom)*.

Before a window can be squeegeed, you must remove the tiny specks of oxidized aluminum deposited on the glass by aluminum screens as well as any paint spatters *(below)*.

For window washing, the most effective cleaner consists of few drops of mild dishwashing detergent in a bucket of warm water.

High Windows and Skylights: Washing the outside of upper-story windows can be done by leaning out the window or using an extension ladder—both risky approaches. A safer alternative is to use telescoping poles *(page 39)*, available at a janitorial supplier.

Skylights can be cleaned only from the roof. Glass skylights can be cleaned with a squeegee in the same way as windows. Acrylic skylights are cared for like acrylic storm windows *(page 33)*.

⚠ **CAUTION** *When using a stepladder to reach a window or chandelier, make sure the braces are all the way down. Never stand on the top step and don't overreach to either side of the ladder.*

 TOOLS

Cotton cloths
Squeegee
Pail
Sponge
Extension pole
    with sponge
    and squeegee
    attachments

GETTING A WINDOW READY TO CLEAN

Before washing a window, remove all paint spatters or gummy residue with a razor-blade scraper with replaceable blades *(right)*. Take care not to damage the wood trim around the window.

Specks from aluminum screens can be removed by washing the window with a solution of one part vinegar in eight parts water, then scrubbing it with a white nylon scouring pad.

To remove labels and decals, warm them with a hair dryer, then scrape them off.

WASHING WINDOWS WITH A SQUEEGEE

Making quick work of small areas.
◆ Sponge on just enough cleaning liquid to wet the entire window, scrubbing any stubborn spots lightly. Then run the sponge around the edges to pick up any loose debris.
◆ Wet the blade of the squeegee and, holding it at an angle, run it lightly across the top of the window to remove the solution from the top inch of the pane.

◆ Pull the squeegee straight down over half of the window (above, left).
◆ Clean the other half of the window by angling the squeegee blade slightly, forcing excess cleaner into the lower corner (above, right).
◆ With a lint-free cloth, wipe off the edges of the glass and the window sill. Let any drops remaining on the pane dry by themselves.

A clean sweep for large windows.
◆ Apply cleaning liquid to the window—a fleece window wand works well (photograph). Sponge off any loose dirt around the edges.
◆ Starting with the squeegee in the top corner, its blade parallel to the sides, pull it across the glass to the opposite edge; then, pivot the squeegee to reverse direction and, without lifting the blade from the glass, continue sweeping from edge to edge until you reach the bottom of the window. Then turn the blade parallel to the bottom and carry the liquid down to the lower edge (right).
◆ Wipe off the edges of the window and the sill with a lint-free cloth.

Using extension poles.
For windows that are too high to reach from the ground, use adjustable aluminum extension poles, which can reach up to 30 feet. Twist the collars of the poles to lock them at the desired length.

Use two poles, if possible, fitting one with a fleece attachment and the other with a squeegee; have a helper handle one of the poles *(left)*. With a single pole, you will have to change fittings constantly, and the liquid may dry during the switch from sponge to squeegee.

MAKING CHANDELIERS SPARKLE

Spraying glass crystals.
◆ Move furniture out from under the chandelier, and spread a plastic drop cloth on the floor.
◆ Turn off the switch serving the chandelier and let the lightbulbs cool.
◆ Working from a ladder or step stool placed to the side of the fixture, tighten the bulbs in their sockets, then spray a chandelier cleaner onto the glass pendants until the liquid begins to drip *(left)*.
◆ Let the chandelier dry, then remove the drop cloth.

Shining Up Porcelain and Tile

Kitchen and bathroom sinks, toilets and bathtubs, and bathroom floors and walls—often made of ceramic tile, porcelain, or porcelain enamel—can usually be kept sparkling with an all-purpose detergent. For tough dirt, use a mild scouring powder with plenty of water. When porcelain or tile becomes stained, stronger remedies are called for *(opposite)*.

Preventing Stains: Rust and minerals in water and pipes can discolor fixtures over time. You can usually solve this problem by installing a whole-house water filter. First have a professional test the water to determine the size and type appropriate for your house. Some homes may need a water softener or water-treatment system; others may

benefit from a simple filter, available at home-improvement centers, that can be attached to the water supply where it enters the house. For copper pipes, use the method pictured below; plastic pipes require similar fittings made of plastic.

Caring for Tile and Grout: A couple of times a year, the grout between tiles needs to be scrubbed *(opposite)*, then sealed. In general, glazed tiles require no special treatment; however, unglazed tiles can be sealed about once a year to prevent staining. The grout and tile can be coated at the same time with a penetrating silicone sealer designed for ceramic tile. Simply apply the sealer with a fleece wax applicator, wipe off the excess, and allow it to dry.

 TOOLS

Fleece wax applicator
Pipe cutter
Wrench
Pail
Cotton cloths
Stiff-bristle brush
Nylon scouring pad
Sponge
Soft-bristle brush
Razor blade
Grout brush

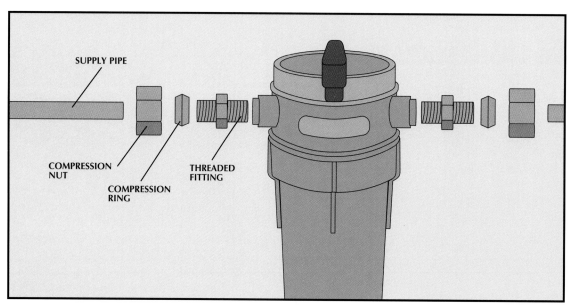

SUPPLY PIPE

COMPRESSION NUT

COMPRESSION RING

THREADED FITTING

Installing a whole-house water filter.
The methods for fitting the filter on your water line will depend on the type of pipe. The following instructions are for copper pipe.
◆ Turn off the water to the house at the main shutoff valve. Open faucets in the house to drain the lines.
◆ Use the template provided with the filter to determine the length of pipe to be removed. With a pipe cutter, cut out

this length of pipe on the house side of the shutoff valve.
◆ Slip a compression ring and a compression nut over the cut ends of the supply pipe.
◆ Screw a threaded fitting into each end of the filter.
◆ Holding the filter in the gap between the cut pipes, tighten the compression nuts with a wrench.

Stains and deposits on both glazed and unglazed surfaces require specific types of cleaners. Always test a solution on a small, inconspicuous spot before proceeding. After using a cleaner, rinse the area with water and dry it off with an absorbent cloth.

Coffee: Dampen a cloth with warm water, dip it in baking soda, and scrub the stain.

Fruit Juice or Tea: Wearing rubber gloves, wash the area with a heavy-duty degreaser. Rinse the spot, then apply a solution of 3 tablespoons laundry bleach in 1 cup warm water.

Grease: Wearing rubber gloves and using a stiff-bristle brush, scrub the affected area with a heavy-duty degreaser. Repeat if necessary.

Hard-Water Scum: Scrub the area with a solution of equal parts vinegar and warm water using a nylon scouring pad; or scrub it with a commercial tub and tile cleaner.

Mildew: Wearing rubber gloves, mix $\frac{1}{2}$ cup laundry bleach with 1 quart water and apply it with a sponge. If the mildew remains, put on goggles and ventilate the room, then use a good commercial mildew remover.

Oil: Mix a thick paste of household scouring powder and water. Apply to the stain and let it stand overnight. Wet dried paste with water and scrub the surface well with a stiff-bristle brush.

Paint: Remove fresh oil-base paint with a cloth dipped in mineral spirits; wear goggles and nitrile gloves and ventilate the area. Wash away the residue with a heavy-duty degreaser. Remove fresh water-base paint with a cloth dampened with warm water and mild dishwashing liquid. Scrub the area with a soft-bristle brush.

Dry paint hardened into thick droplets can be scraped off with a single-edge razor blade. Then, wearing nitrile gloves and goggles and ventilating the area, remove the remaining paint with lacquer thinner.

Rubber-Heel Marks: Wearing nitrile gloves and goggles and providing the area with good ventilation, dab the marks off with a cloth dipped in mineral spirits.

Rust: Rub light stains with a cut lemon, then wash the area with mild dishwashing detergent. Remove dark stains with a solution of 1 part oxalic acid and 20 parts water—wear goggles and nitrile gloves when handling the powdered acid. Wash the solution off immediately with water. Repeat if necessary. Alternatively, you can use a commercial scouring powder containing oxalic acid.

Soap Scum: Wearing rubber gloves, apply a heavy-duty degreaser and allow it to soak for 10 minutes. Then scrub the surface with a stiff-bristle brush or a white nylon scrub pad.

Unknown Stain: On glazed tile or porcelain, apply a stiff paste of ammonia (wear rubber gloves and ventilate the area) and an absorbent powder such as whiting (calcium carbonate), talcum powder, or cornstarch; let it stand for one hour, then wash it off with soapy water. On porous surfaces, mix scouring powder with water to make a slurry, and mop it over the area. Let the solution stand for about 5 minutes, and then scrub the surface vigorously with a stiff-bristle brush.

⚠ **CAUTION** *To avoid the possibility of spontaneous combustion, store rags soaked in mineral spirits or lacquer thinner in tightly sealed containers or spread them outdoors to dry.*

CARING FOR GROUT

Scrubbing and sealing grout.
◆ Make a paste of water and a mildly abrasive scouring powder.
◆ Dip a grout brush in the paste and gently scrub the joints *(right)*.
◆ Rinse off the paste and wipe the surface with a clean, white, lint-free cloth and let it dry.
◆ Moisten a second cloth with silicone grout sealer and wipe it along the grout joints, rewetting the cloth as needed. Wipe off any sealer that gets onto the tiles.
◆ Let the surface dry for 24 hours.

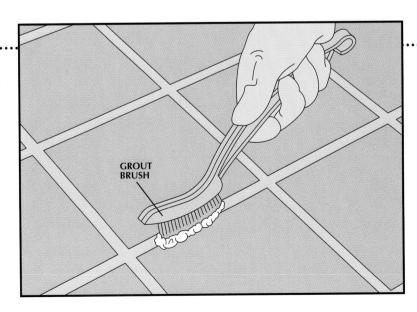

GROUT BRUSH

Brightening Walls and Ceilings

The type of covering on a wall or ceiling dictates the method used to clean it.

Spot Removal: Before tackling individual spots on a wall or ceiling, consider what effect cleaning isolated spots will have on the surface. Obliterating a highly visible smudge may leave a clean mark on an otherwise dingy wall. You may then have to clean the whole wall.

Preparing Surfaces: Before washing an entire wall or ceiling, pull all of the furniture away from the walls, and cover it and the floor with drop cloths. Take down pictures, curtains, and blinds; tape plastic over metal fixtures such as chandeliers or wall sconces to protect them from damage by cleaning chemicals. Then vacuum the walls, ceiling, baseboard, and door and window trim, paying special attention to corners, grooves, and patterns in the woodwork.

Paint and Wallpaper: Flat and enamel paints and vinyl- and vinyl-coated papers can be cleaned using water with general-purpose detergent *(opposite)*. A solution of 1 part chlorine bleach to 1 part warm water will eliminate mildew; avoid splashing the bleach on carpeting or clothing.

Wall coverings made of paper cannot be washed. Dust or vacuum them instead, then clean them with a special tool called a dry sponge *(below)*; while this removes the film of dirt, it will not lift fingerprints. Certain paints and acoustic tile can also be cleaned this way. If you aren't sure whether your walls are washable, test a small, inconspicuous area.

⚠️ **CAUTION** *When using a stepladder, make sure the spreader braces are all the way down. Never stand on the top step and don't overreach to either side of the ladder.*

TOOLS

Vacuum
Dry wallpaper
  sponge
Pails
C-clamps
Sponges
Cotton cloths

Cleaning nonwashable surfaces.
Fold a dry sponge *(photograph)* in half and rub it gently over the surface in slightly overlapping strokes *(right)*. When one surface of the sponge is soiled, refold it to expose a clean section. When all the surfaces of the sponge are dirty, replace it with a clean one.

Wiping down washable surfaces.

◆ Set up a stepladder so you can reach the ceiling without fully extending your arm. Place two pails—one empty, one containing cleaning solution—on the ladder shelf. If necessary, clamp a board to the shelf to support the buckets.

◆ Dip a sponge in the cleaner and wring it out. Wipe the cleaner over as wide an area of the ceiling as you can safely reach (above). Wring out the sponge in the empty pail, then sponge off the softened dirt; wring the sponge again. Dry the area with a soft cloth.

◆ Reposition the ladder and continue until you have scrubbed the entire ceiling.

◆ For the walls, wash the dirtiest areas—over heat registers, near light switches, and around picture frames. Then, starting in a corner and just above the baseboard, wash a 3-foot-wide strip up the wall to the ceiling, working in overlapping vertical and horizontal strokes. Immediately wipe the strip with a cloth, working from ceiling to floor in order to remove streaks and drip marks. Continue cleaning adjacent strips until you have circled the room.

◆ Wipe the baseboards and the framing around doors and windows with a damp cloth, then wash them, if necessary, the same way as the walls and ceiling.

TRICKS OF THE TRADE

Removing Tape Effortlessly

To loosen adhesive tape stuck to the wall, hold a clean white cloth over the tape and press it with a warm iron (right). Then gently peel back the tape.

Caring for Textiles

Household fabrics including carpets, curtains, and upholstery need regular cleaning to stay fresh looking. When it comes to tackling spills and spots, a methodical approach works best. As this chapter shows, it takes the appropriate cleaner and cleaning method to rescue fabrics from stains.

A Methodical Approach to Removing Spots   46

Soaking Up Fresh Spills
Testing a Cleaner
Working on the Stain

Rejuvenating Rugs and Carpets   52

Raising Depressions in Carpeting
Brushing Pile Before and After Cleaning
Hand-Washing an Area Rug
Dry-Cleaning with Powder
Extracting Dirt with Hot Water
Repairing Damaged Carpet

Lifting Soil from Upholstery   59

Shampooing Furniture
Restoring Vinyl and Leather

Performing a spot test →

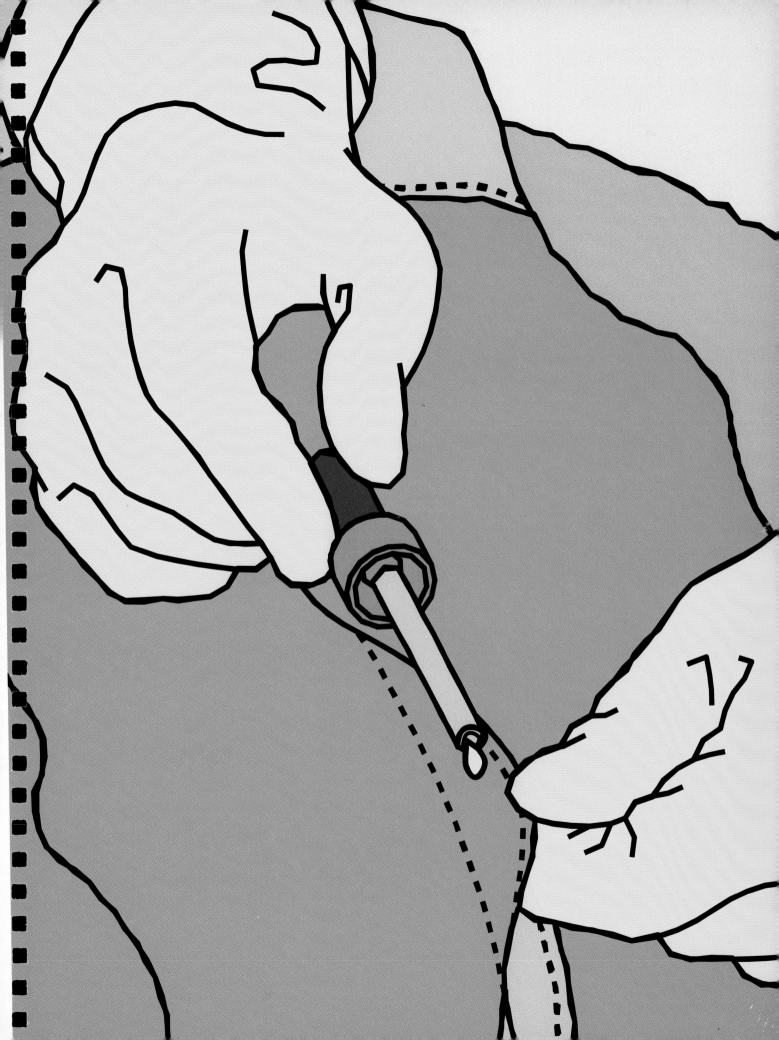

Household textiles come in a multiplicity of weaves, textures, and fibers, each with properties that affect how the material responds to soil and how the soil is removed *(pages 116-117)*. Before treating an item, examine its label, if there is one. Entrust to a professional fabrics that require dry cleaning. Tackle spots on washables with the appropriate cleaning agent or take them to a dry cleaner.

Removing Stains: Spots you treat immediately are the easiest to remove. Often you can draw off a spill with an absorbent powder or by a simple process called wicking *(opposite)*. For an older stain, first try to identify the substance that caused it, observing its look, feel, or smell. Then refer to the chart on pages 118 to 121 to select an appropriate cleaning agent. Starting with the first product on the list, apply it as described on pages 49 to 51. (On upholstery, however, use only blotting, to avoid overwetting the backing material.) If the first product does not remove the spot, continue along the list of cleaning agents until the stain is gone. For convenience, keep a stock of cleaners on hand *(below)*.

Cleaning Techniques: Before treating a fabric, test the chemical—or water—on an inconspicuous part to make sure it won't be damaged. Always blot or tamp the item lightly—do not rub—and work on the reverse side of the material whenever possible. Detergents and chemical solvents need time to act—several light applications usually produce better results than a single heavy inundation. Allow dry-cleaning fluid, amyl acetate, and acetone to evaporate before applying the next product. Rinse out other agents before moving to the next.

TOOLS

Spoon
White cotton cloths
Dull knife
Eye dropper
Small soft-bristle brush
Pail

A HANDY CLEANING KIT

A well-stocked kit of cleaning agents is the best defense against the spots that mar household fabrics. With the right solution, and a white cotton cloth to apply it, you are well poised to lift spills before they can set. Assemble all the cleaning agents you may need in the same place, but keep them in their original bottles, which are properly labeled with safety and disposal instructions.

Include the following chemicals in your kit: dry-cleaning fluid, amyl acetate, acetone, a mild colorless liquid detergent, white vinegar, and ammonia. You'll also want an enzyme detergent designed for soaking spots before washing, a dye remover, and either oxalic acid or a rust-removal product designed for fabric.

For soaking up spills, keep a small plastic bag filled with an absorbent powder such as cornstarch, cornmeal, or talcum powder.

Absorbing grease.
◆ Immediately after a spill, cover the entire spot with a $\frac{1}{4}$-inch-thick layer of absorbent powder *(left)*.
◆ Leave the powder in place for 1 minute; then remove it by shaking it off onto a piece of newspaper or picking it up with a spoon, taking care not to rub the powder into the fabric.
◆ Repeat the process with fresh layers of powder as long as it continues to absorb traces of the spill. Then remove the stain *(pages 48-51)*.

Wicking out fluid.
While a spill is still wet, lightly touch the tip of a crumpled absorbent white cloth or paper towel to the spot *(right)*; the liquid will be drawn into the cloth or paper by capillary action. Do not push down on the fabric; this could force the liquid into the fibers or spread the stain.

For solid substances, lightly scrape the surface with a dull knife to remove the matter. Then dilute the residue with an appropriate cleaner *(pages 118-121)* and wick it out as described above. Remove the stain *(pages 48-51)*.

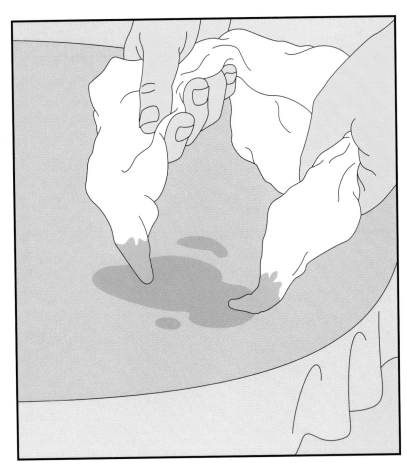

Hardening Gum with Ice

Put an ice cube in a plastic bag and press the ice against the gum, holding it there until the entire wad becomes brittle. Slide the edge of a stainless-steel spoon between the frozen gum and the fabric and pry it loose. Treat any remaining spot with the appropriate stain-removal agents *(pages 118-121)*.

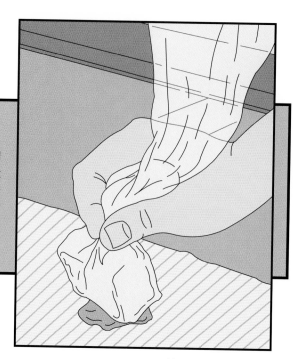

TESTING A CLEANER

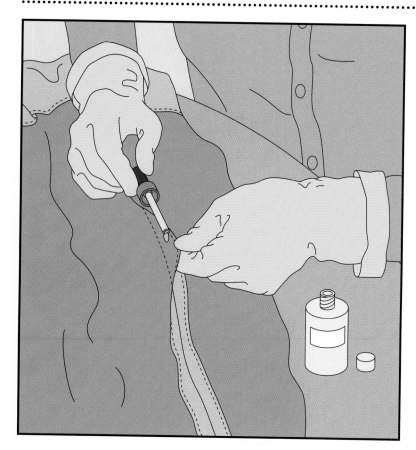

Performing a spot test.
◆ With an eye dropper, apply several drops of the stain remover to an inconspicuous area of the fabric, such as a seam allowance *(left)*.
◆ Blot the solution with a clean white cloth, pressing it down firmly for 30 seconds. If the cloth has picked up color from the fabric, the color bleeds or changes, or you notice damage to the fiber, rinse out the cleaner quickly with water if it is a water-base product, blot out the moisture, and try a different solution in another area. When none of these conditions is present, simply rinse out a water-base cleaner with water and blot up the moisture. For non-water-base cleaner, let the moisture evaporate instead of rinsing it out.

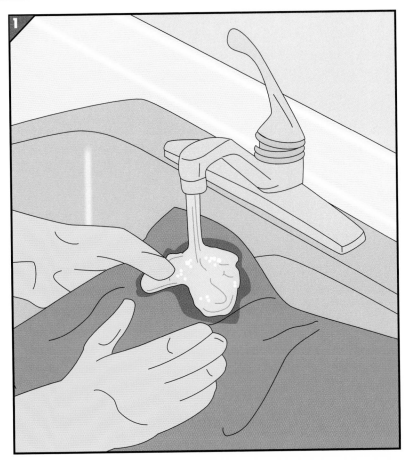

1. Flooding with water.

◆ Where water is the appropriate cleaning agent *(pages 118-121)*, hold the affected area under a running tap of lukewarm water *(left)*. Avoid hot water, which can set the stain, and do not rub the fabric.

◆ Let the material dry. If the spot is still apparent, move to Step 2.

2. Blotting on the cleaning agent.

◆ Place the affected area of fabric stained-side down over several layers of absorbent white cloth laid on top of a flat, nonabsorbent surface—such as the bottom of a glass baking dish.

◆ Moisten the stained area lightly with the stain-removal agent, then blot the blemish lightly with the corner of a white cloth *(right)*. Reposition the cloths under the fabric frequently to keep a clean section beneath the stain.

For upholstery, moisten a white cloth and squeeze it almost dry before blotting on the cleaning agent to avoid saturating the lining or backing.

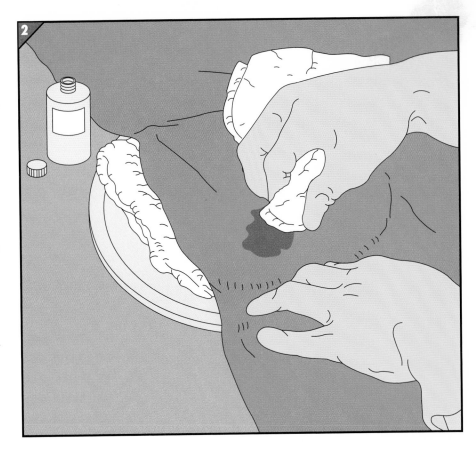

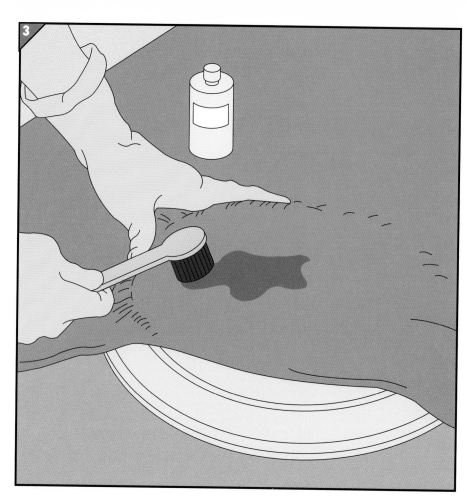

3. Tamping the cleaner.
◆ Lay the fabric face down on a hard, flat, nonabsorbent surface, such as a glass baking dish.
◆ Moisten the area with the stain-removal agent.
◆ Gently tap the spot with a small and clean soft-bristle brush, such as a shoe-polish brush or toothbrush, moistened with the stain-removal agent.
◆ Blot the fabric occasionally with a white cloth and keep tapping with the brush until as much of the stain is removed as possible.

4. Flushing out the stain.
◆ Lay the fabric stained-side down on cloths as for blotting *(page 49)*.
◆ Trickle a very small amount of cleaning solution onto the spot *(right)* and wait for the cloth under the fabric to absorb the liquid.
◆ Change the position of the absorbent cloth to provide a clean area beneath the stain, and repeat the process. If you are applying chlorine bleach, let it sit for no more than two minutes. You can leave other types of bleach on fabric for up to 15 minutes.
◆ Allow dry-cleaning fluid, amyl acetate, and acetone to evaporate completely before trying the next product. For any other product, rinse it out *(Step 5)*.

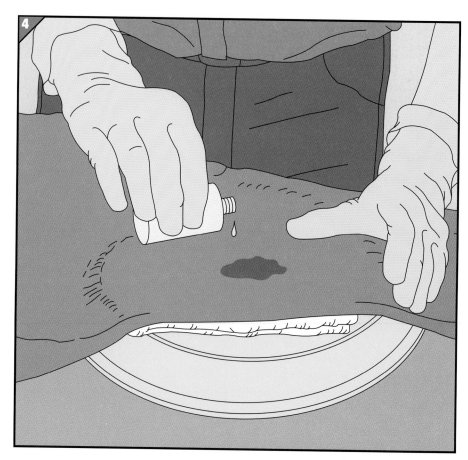

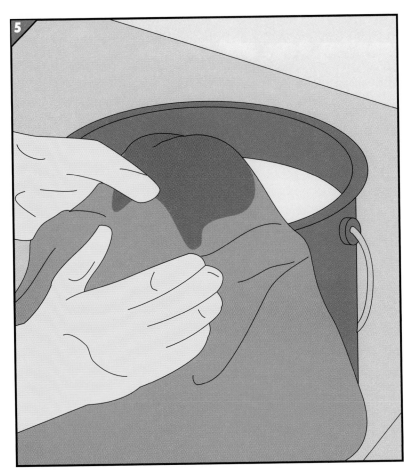

5. Rinsing.

◆ Fill a small pail or bowl with water.

◆ Swish the affected area of the fabric in the water. Then change the water and swish it again. Repeat the process a third time.

◆ Let the fabric dry. If the stain has not disappeared completely, try the next stain-removal agent.

DEALING WITH PET STAINS

The trick to removing urine from carpets is rapid response—immediately soak up as much liquid as possible with paper towels, being careful not to spread the stain. Then, place an absorbent cloth over the area and put pressure on it with your foot (right). To dispel the odor, you can use a deodorizing cleaner made for the purpose.

For dried stains, an effective remedy is to apply a bacterial enzyme digester—a product that breaks down the organic material. Work the solution into the carpet. Let it sit for the specified time; then, if required, scrub out the residue with a damp sponge.

To deal with excrement, lift off loose material with your hand in a plastic bag. Soak the spot with water and gently rub any dried material. Then apply a bacterial enzyme digester.

For vomit, scrape up as much as possible with two pieces of cardboard. Then apply an absorbent powder and let it sit for a few minutes. Scoop up the material, rinse the area, and apply a bacterial enzyme digester.

If any stain remains after these treatments, clean the spot as recommended on pages 118 to 121.

Even with frequent vacuuming, rugs and carpets eventually lose their brightness and springy nap. Most manufacturers recommend deep cleaning them at least once a year to help restore color and texture. With the possible exception of a fragile antique or a delicate silk oriental—which should be entrusted to a professional—almost any rug or carpet can be deep cleaned safely. Damaged tufts in carpeting can be replaced *(pages 57-58)*.

Cleaning Methods: The easiest way to wash a small rug is to scrub it by hand outdoors *(pages 54-55)*. For lightly soiled wall-to-wall carpets or those containing dyes that are not colorfast, the preferred method is dry cleaning with a solvent-impregnated absorbent powder *(page 56)*. For heavier soil, the most common method is hot-water extraction—also known as steam cleaning—with a mild detergent *(page 57)*.

Carpets that have been treated with an absorbent powder are ready for use immediately. Allow those that have been steamed to dry for several hours (up to 48 hours in humid weather).

Testing the Cleaner: Before applying a liquid cleaning agent, even plain water, check it for compatibility with the rug or carpet. Even mild detergents can sometimes cause dyes to dull and bleed. Rug and carpet manufacturers often specify the appropriate cleaning agent on a label. In the absence of such a label, test the proposed cleaner on an inconspicuous spot or unravel a few strands of yarn from a scrap of the same carpet and soak them for a few hours in the cleaning agent. Allow the test fibers to dry before you compare them with the untested fibers.

Preparing the Carpet: Before cleaning a carpet, remove as much furniture as possible and wrap the legs of the remaining pieces with aluminum foil to prevent them from staining the damp carpet and to protect the furniture from the cleaner. Vacuum the carpet—both sides of an area rug—and remove any stains *(pages 46-51)* to keep them from spreading during cleaning. Brush carpeting to lift compacted pile and help expose deeply embedded dirt *(opposite)*.

Cleaning Equipment: Carpet-cleaning machines can be obtained from rental agencies, dry cleaners, and supermarkets; these sources also carry the cleaning agents formulated for use with the machines. Ask for any special instructions that apply to the machine you rent. If you expect to clean your carpets frequently, consider buying a model intended for home use.

TOOLS

Vacuum	Towels
Steam iron	Powder-brushing
Cotton cloth	machine
Stiff-bristle broom	Hot-water
Pail	extraction machine
Soft-bristle brush	Scissors
1 x 4 and handle	Tweezers
for squeegee	Carpet
	"cookie cutter"
	Putty knife

TIPS TO KEEP CARPETS FRESH

By adhering to a program of routine maintenance, you can lengthen the interval between deep cleanings. Weekly treatment with a vacuum or a lightweight carpet sweeper *(photograph)*, focused on high-traffic areas, prevents dirt from becoming embedded. Door-mats protect wall-to-wall carpets from tracked-in dirt and area rugs catch spills around coffee tables. Stains and spots in carpets are less likely to set when removed immediately *(pages 46-51)*. Shifting furniture an inch or so each week can prevent the pile beneath the legs from being permanently crushed. When such depressions cannot be brushed out by hand, remove the indentations as described opposite.

RAISING DEPRESSIONS IN CARPETING

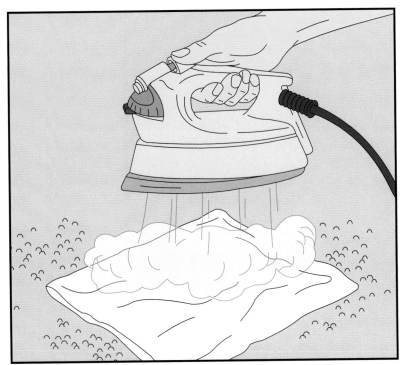

Steaming out indentations.
◆ Raise the crushed carpet tufts with the edge of a coin.
◆ Lay a clean white cotton cloth over the indentation and, holding a steam iron set at medium heat 3 or 4 inches above the spot, apply steam to the cloth until the crushed yarn is restored to its upright position *(left)*.

BRUSHING PILE BEFORE AND AFTER CLEANING

Lifting the pile.
◆ Determine the nap direction by brushing the pile so the tufts stand upright.
◆ Pull a stiff-bristle broom toward you against the nap direction in overlapping strokes, working across the entire carpet until the pile is uniform *(right)*. Or you can move a vacuum cleaner with a beater bar against the nap direction.

1. Preparing the rug.
◆ Indoors, vacuum both sides of the rug and test it for color-fastness *(page 52)*.
◆ Outdoors, clean an area of concrete patio or drive-way large enough to accom-modate the rug.
◆ Lay the rug face down on the prepared area and wet it thoroughly with a garden hose *(left)*.

2. Scrubbing the backing.
◆ Prepare a mild carpet detergent in a pail and, starting near the center of the rug, scrub in wide, circular strokes with a soft-bristle brush, lathering an area about 2 feet square *(right)*.
◆ After scrubbing a few overlapping areas, rinse away the lather.
◆ Continue scrubbing and rinsing, work-ing from the center of the rug out to the edges. Prepare a new batch of detergent when the suds become gray or sediment accumulates in the bottom of the pail.

3. Cleaning the fringe.

◆ With the rug still face down, hold the strands from underneath and brush them with the detergent from the edge of the rug and working out *(left)*.

◆ When you have cleaned the fringe along one edge, rinse it before scrubbing the next.

For an extremely dirty section, prepare a slightly stronger detergent mixture and rub the fringe back and forth between your hands before brushing it out.

4. Rinsing the rug.

◆ Rinse the backing and fringe with the hose, beginning at the center and working out to the edges *(above, left)*. Keep rinsing until the suds disappear.

◆ Turn the rug over and clean the upper surface *(Steps 1-3)*.

◆ Rinse the rug again, this time with a helper removing some of the water with a wooden squeegee—a short, smooth piece of 1-by-4 attached to a handle. Pull the squeegee from the center of the rug toward the edges *(above, right)*; stop short of the fringes.

For a small rug, blot up the water with terry-cloth towels.

◆ Dry the rug on a clothesline or lay it, face up, on a dry lawn out of the sun. While the pile is still slightly damp, brush it *(page 53)*. Move the rug occasionally to avoid suffocating the grass.

DRY-CLEANING WITH POWDER

1. Spreading powder.
Spread carpet-cleaning powder, 1 cup at a time, over the surface of the carpet, holding the container about 1 foot above the floor. Use a throwing motion to distribute the powder evenly and heavily without mounds *(left)*. Unless the manufacturer's instructions specify otherwise, spread 5 pounds of powder for every 100 square feet of carpet.

2. Working in the powder.
◆ Starting at a corner of the carpet, pull a powder-brushing machine backward along one edge, then push it forward in a pass that slightly overlaps the first. Continue working back and forth in this manner until you reach the opposite edge *(right)*.
◆ Go back over the carpet at least twice in this same pattern. Then, turn the machine 90 degrees and repeat the process.
◆ Turn the machine 90 degrees again and make a final sweep back and forth across the carpet so each pass is in the direction opposite to the first brushing. Sprinkle more powder as you go on any area not thoroughly coated.
◆ Let the powder sit for about two hours, or until it changes color from light brown to almost white. Then, vacuum the carpet very slowly, working in the same pattern you used to brush the powder in.

EXTRACTING DIRT WITH HOT WATER

Steam-cleaning a carpet.
◆ Fill the detergent tank with cleaning solution and connect the pressure and extraction hoses to the machine.
◆ Starting on the side of the room opposite the door, hold the cleaning wand with the suction nozzle flush against the carpet and move it back and forth across a 3-foot square in a zigzag pattern. On each backward stroke, squeeze the grip lever to spray cleaning solution *(right)*; release the lever on the forward strokes, allowing the vacuum action to extract dirty water. Make no more than three passes.
◆ Change the stroke direction slightly and go over the square again, using only the extractor on both the forward and backward strokes.
◆ Clean adjacent areas of carpet, slightly overlapping the edges of the squares and working back and forth across the carpet until you have reached the opposite side. Refill the detergent tank when it is empty. Do not reuse the extracted solution; it contains dirt that can clog the nozzle.
◆ When the entire carpet has been cleaned, brush the damp pile to raise the nap *(page 53)*.

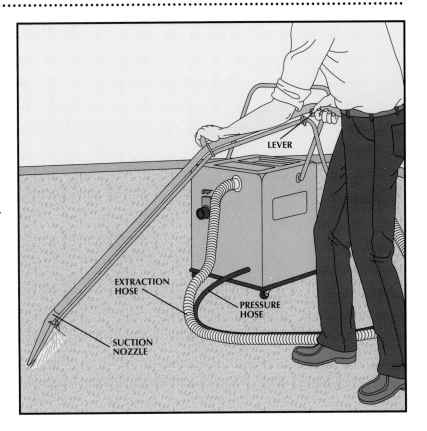

LEVER

EXTRACTION HOSE

PRESSURE HOSE

SUCTION NOZZLE

REPAIRING DAMAGED CARPET

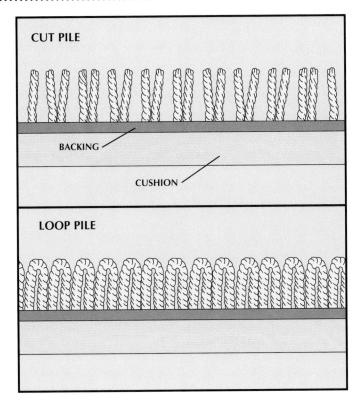

CUT PILE

BACKING

CUSHION

LOOP PILE

Determining the type of pile.
The method you use for replacing burnt or marred tufts depends on the type of pile. A carpet has either a cut-pile or a looped-pile surface. With cut pile, the tufts have been trimmed, leaving a surface of cut ends *(left, top)*. With looped pile, the exposed ends of the tufts are left as closed loops *(left, bottom)*.

Trim slightly damaged tufts in cut pile carefully with sharp scissors. If necessary, a few tufts can be cut out and replaced *(page 58, top)*. However, if tufts in looped pile are damaged, or if more than a few tufts in cut pile are affected, cut out and replace a small section of carpet *(page 58, bottom)*. When using a cookie-cutter tool, your approach will depend on whether the carpet has a cushioned backing glued to the floor, or a separate cushion laid under the carpet.

Replacing individual tufts.

◆ Trim off each damaged tuft at its base with small, sharp scissors.
◆ With tweezers, pull relacement tufts out of a remnant or from an inconspicuous spot such as a closet.

◆ Dab latex adhesive on the end of the replacement tuft.
◆ Grasping the tuft with tweezers *(above)*, set it into a hole in the carpet backing, pushing it in far enough to seat the base of the tuft securely.

Restoring a small section.

◆ To use a cookie cutter tool *(photograph)* on a carpet with a separate cushion, set the tool's depth adjustment dial to cut through only the carpet and its backing.
◆ Center the cutter over the damaged area. Press down, turning the tool in one direction, then in the other to cut through the carpet *(below)*. Pull out the cut section.
◆ Cut a piece of burlap 2 inches larger than the removed section and slip it into the opening under the surrounding carpet.
◆ Glue the burlap to the underside of the carpet with latex adhesive *(inset)*.

◆ Cut a replacement section from a carpet remnant, spread adhesive on the burlap, and press the section into place, freeing any caught tufts with tweezers.
◆ Dab off any stray adhesive, then place a weight on the patch until the adhesive sets.
◆ Gently rub any flattened pile to raise it.

If the carpet has an attached cushion, set the cookie cutter to cut right through the cushion. With a small putty knife, scrape any of the cushion and adhesive from the floor. Apply a thin bead of latex adhesive to the floor and around the edges of the replacement piece, then press the piece into place.

BACKING

BURLAP

CUSHION

Like carpets and other fabrics, upholstery collects dust and grime. Once-a-week vacuuming will help keep it bright and fresh looking. Clean it once a year to get rid of deep-seated dirt.

Vacuuming: Remove and vacuum loose cushions and pillows, then vacuum the piece of furniture, using the upholstery brush and crevice tool in seams and around cording and buttons. Do not remove cushion covers or slipcovers for separate machine washing. Instead, leave them on to be shampooed with the piece of furniture; if covers are machine washed, they may shrink or stretch out of alignment.

Cleaning: Before shampooing an item of furniture, determine if the fabric is washable. Check the manufacturer's label, which may be sewn to the underside of the cushions or stapled to the frame. Except for cotton, most fabrics can be shampooed with detergent; use either a homemade cleaner *(below and pages 60-61)* or commercial upholstery shampoo. When shampooing a piece of furniture, apply only the foam from the detergent—not the liquid—to avoid soaking the piece. If the fabric is cotton or cannot be washed, have the furniture drycleaned by a professional. Clean leather and vinyl with mild detergent *(page 61)*.

TOOLS

Vacuum
Pails
Eggbeater
Kitchen tongs
Terry towels
Soft-bristle nylon
   scrub brush
Cotton cloths
Spray bottle
Sponge

SHAMPOOING FURNITURE

1. Preparing the cleaner.
◆ Mix 1 gallon of lukewarm water with 1 tablespoon of clear or white dishwashing detergent.
◆ Pour about 1 quart of the solution into a pail. With an eggbeater or an electric mixer, whip the ingredients until most of the solution becomes a stiff foam *(right)*.
◆ Test the cleaning solution on an inconspicuous area of the upholstery—the underside, a hem, or a seam allowance *(page 48)*.

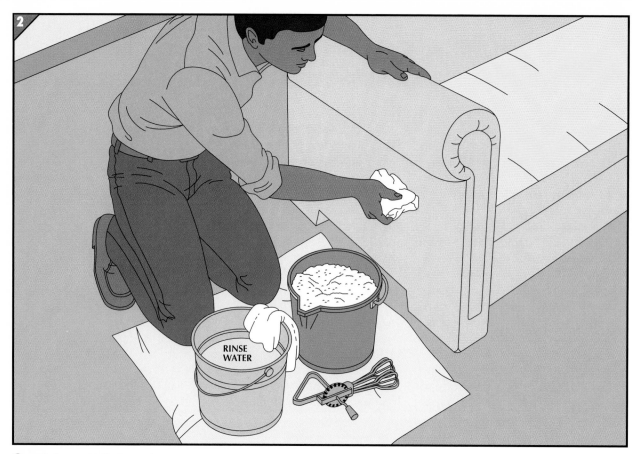

2. Wiping off light soil.

◆ Fold a clean white terry towel into a pad and dip it into the foam. Wring it until you squeeze out all the liquid.

◆ Wipe one complete panel of the upholstery with firm, parallel strokes, overlapping them slightly *(above)*. Occasionally dip the towel into the pail for more foam, wringing it each time. As the towel gets dirty, refold it to expose a clean surface. When the foam in the pail begins to dissolve, whip it again.

◆ Repeat the process, going over the panel at right angles to the original strokes.

◆ Remove the detergent by wiping the panel with a clean terry towel moistened in fresh water and wrung dry. Work parallel to the first cleaning strokes; rinse the towel often, wringing it dry each time.

3. Brushing out heavy soil.

◆ Using a pair of kitchen tongs, immerse a nylon scrub brush with very soft bristles in boiling water for a few seconds to soften the bristles even more. Blot it dry with a clean terry towel.

◆ Dip the brush in the foam, then shake most of it back into the pail.

◆ Pressing lightly, scrub the upholstery in a circular pattern over 1 square foot of fabric at a time *(right)*. Scrub adjacent areas, overlapping the areas slightly.

◆ Dip the brush into the foam as necessary, and when the bristles begin to stiffen, immerse them in boiling water. If the foam begins to dissolve, whip it again.

◆ Remove the detergent from the upholstery with a clean terry towel as you did in Step 2.

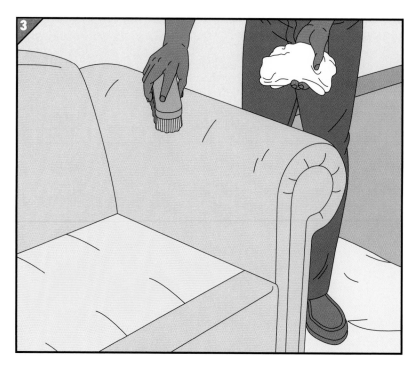

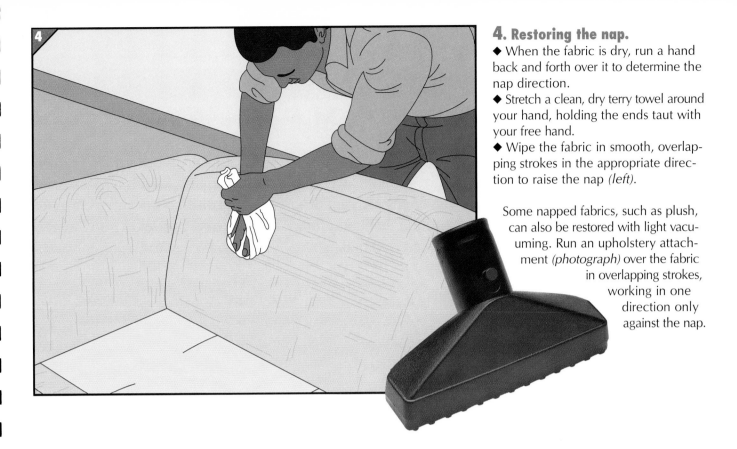

4. Restoring the nap.
◆ When the fabric is dry, run a hand back and forth over it to determine the nap direction.
◆ Stretch a clean, dry terry towel around your hand, holding the ends taut with your free hand.
◆ Wipe the fabric in smooth, overlapping strokes in the appropriate direction to raise the nap *(left)*.

Some napped fabrics, such as plush, can also be restored with light vacuuming. Run an upholstery attachment *(photograph)* over the fabric in overlapping strokes, working in one direction only against the nap.

RESTORING VINYL AND LEATHER

Wiping the furniture.
◆ To determine if the furniture is leather or vinyl, unzip a cushion cover and check the back—leather has a suedelike surface.
◆ Mix $\frac{1}{8}$ cup clear or white dishwashing detergent in 1 quart of water. Moisten a cloth with the solution and dab it on an inconspicuous spot. Let the cleaner dry and check for damage to the material.
◆ If the solution is safe, apply it to leather with a wrung-out sponge. For vinyl, pour the solution into a spray bottle and lightly mist the material.
◆ Wipe the furniture dry with a white lint-free cloth.

Special Cleaning Problems

In addition to daily or weekly house-cleaning chores, there are other jobs you will have to tackle periodically, such as attending to kitchen and laundry appliances, cleaning or replacing air filters, or vacuuming and scrubbing a swimming pool. And in the event of a plumbing leak or a flood, a house may require a good deal of time and effort to restore it to normal.

Taking Care of Household Appliances   **64**

Keeping a Refrigerator Fresh and Clean
Dealing with a Ceramic Cooktop
Cleaning the Insides of an Electric Range
Getting at the Interior of a Gas Stove
Emptying the Lint Trap in a Clothes Washer
Maintaining Airflow through a Dryer
Sanitizing a Trash Compactor
Detaching a Dishwasher Filter for Cleaning

Attending to Air Filters   **75**

Servicing a Range Hood
Caring for Room Air Conditioners
Tending to the Furnace
Servicing Electronic Filters

Keeping Swimming Pools Clean and Clear   **79**

Checking the Chemical Balance
How a Pool Refreshes Itself
Clearing Out Debris
Flushing a Filter
Scrubbing Concrete with Acid

Dealing with the Aftermath of a Flood   **84**

Turning Off the Power
Draining a Ceiling
Getting Rid of Standing Water
Draining Walls
Removing Wet Wall Material
Quick-Drying with Fresh Air

Cleaning a gas burner →

Taking Care of Household Appliances

Virtually all the appliances in your home need periodic cleaning. With routine attention such as the practices suggested in the chart below, they will require extensive cleanings less often. The methods shown on the following pages are common to most models. Check your owner's manual for parts of an appliance that may need special attention.

Moving Appliances: Most machines can be pulled out from the wall to provide access under and behind them. For one equipped with wheels or rollers, pull it straight out to prevent damaging the floor, or roll it onto hardboard. Appliances without wheels can be walked out from the wall or shifted onto hardboard. To move a range away from the wall, open the oven door slightly and grasp the top of the door frame in both hands. Gas appliances with flexible gas lines can be moved, but do so carefully to avoid rupturing connections.

Cleaning Tools and Products: A handy tool for cleaning appliances is a special brush resembling a bottle brush with a long, flexible handle, available at appliance parts suppliers. A mild detergent is the best cleaner for any appliance, inside and out. Mix 1 tablespoon of detergent in 1 gallon of warm water; do not prepare a stronger solution—the sticky residue will be difficult to rinse away. For baked-on grease that detergent cannot remove, use a heavy-duty degreaser. For tougher grime on enamel and most metal surfaces, use oven cleaner or $\frac{1}{2}$ cup of sudsy ammonia in 1 gallon of warm water, but avoid applying these products to aluminum or painted surfaces. To kill odors, dissolve 2 tablespoons of baking soda in 1 quart of water. Rinse off the solution with water; left behind, the residue will trap dirt. For spots on plastic and painted surfaces, use a white nylon pad; avoid abrasive powders, which can dull the finish. For metal and porcelain enamel, #1/0 steel wool is best.

 TOOLS

White nylon
   scouring pad
Steel wool (#1/0)
Toothbrush
Cotton cloths
Sponges
Long-handled
   appliance brush
Vacuum cleaner
Razor-blade scraper
Screwdriver

APPLIANCE UPKEEP

Refrigerators and freezers	Keep door gaskets clean; dirt can interfere with the seal. Wipe down the interior with a solution of baking powder and water and put open boxes of baking powder inside to absorb odors. Clean the refrigerator drain and drain pan twice a year to keep odors from developing *(opposite)*. Brush dirt off condenser coils twice a year to keep the appliance operating efficiently *(page 66)*. Defrost freezers when the ice is 1 inch thick.
Ranges	Wipe down the cooktop regularly. Clean the insides as needed *(pages 67-70)*, but for a self-cleaning oven follow the instructions for the model.
Microwave ovens	Sponge spatters off the interior with detergent immediately after use.
Clothes washers	Mop up spilled laundry products immediately. Unless the machine has a self-cleaning filter, clean out the lint trap after each load *(page 71)*.
Clothes dryers	Clean the lint trap after every load *(pages 71-72)* and the exhaust system twice a year *(page 72)*.
Trash compactors	Rinse out containers before depositing them in the compactor. Periodically remove the drawer for cleaning *(page 73)*.
Garbage disposers	Always operate the disposer with plenty of water to flush it completely.
Dishwashers	Wipe the edges of the door and frame regularly. Unless the machine has a self-cleaning filter, clean the filter after each load *(page 74)*, and check the sink air vent periodically for debris.

Cleaning the drain tube.
◆ Pull out the crisper drawers.
◆ If the refrigerator has a drain in the interior floor, remove the plastic drain cap.
◆ Sprinkle baking soda on a moistened toothbrush and scrub the drain *(left)*.
◆ Pour clean water into the drain to rinse it.

Washing drain pans.
Drain pans may be located either at the bottom front of the refrigerator or in the back above the compressor.
◆ For a pan at the front, open the refrigerator door, if necessary, and snap out the grille from the bottom front.
◆ Slide out the drain pan *(right)*.
◆ Wash the pan with detergent and warm water.

For a drain pan at the back of the refrigerator *(inset)*, simply wipe the pan clean with a damp cloth.

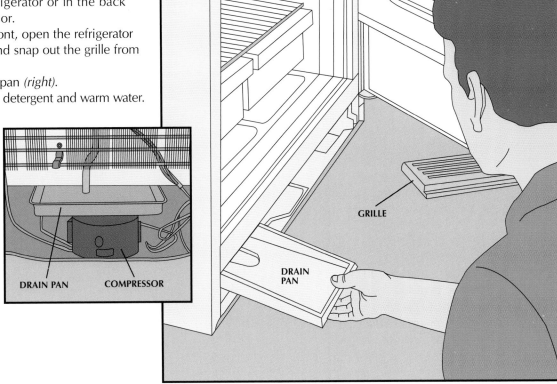

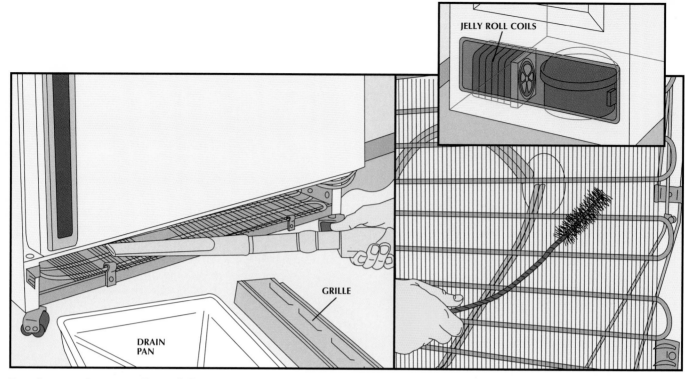

JELLY ROLL COILS

GRILLE

DRAIN PAN

Dusting condenser coils and fins.

The condenser coils and metal fins that disperse the heat from a refrigerator are usually located at the bottom front or the rear of the appliance. Before cleaning them, unplug the power cord.

To expose coils and fins at the bottom front of a refrigerator, snap off the floor-level grille below the door and remove the drain pan. With a long-handled brush, dust the coils and

fins. Vacuum up debris with a crevice tool *(above, left)*.

For coils and fins at the back, move the appliance away from the wall and brush off coils and fins *(above, right)*, or use a vacuum cleaner with upholstery-brush attachment.

For "jelly roll" style coils *(inset)*—accessible from the back of the refrigerator—bend a long-handled appliance brush into an L shape to reach the coils.

DEALING WITH A CERAMIC COOKTOP

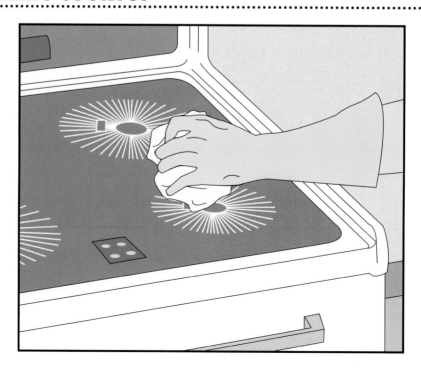

Cleaning the cooktop.

◆ For routine cleaning, rub a small amount of cleaning cream made for ceramic cooktops onto the cooktop with a dry clean cloth or paper towel *(right)*. Wipe the surface clean.
◆ For baked-on spills, rub a small amount of cream onto the material, then scrape it away with a razor-blade scraper.

CLEANING THE INSIDES OF AN ELECTRIC RANGE

1. Removing the accessories.
◆ Unplug the stove or shut off the power at the service panel.
◆ Lift each heating element and pull the electrical contacts out of the receptacles under the cooktop. If the elements lift up easily at one side, they are not removable; simply tip them up out of the way.
◆ Remove the drip pans *(right)*, trim rings, and any accessories such as control knobs.
◆ Wash all parts except the heating elements in a detergent solution. For lingering dirt, put on rubber gloves and apply a heavy-duty degreaser, then rinse with a damp sponge.

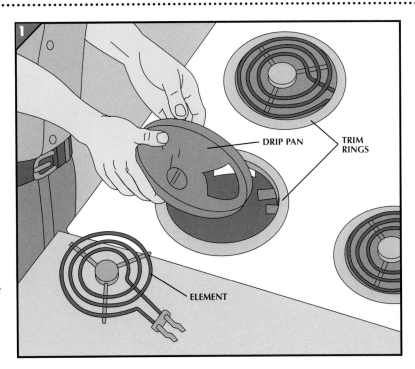

DRIP PAN

TRIM RINGS

ELEMENT

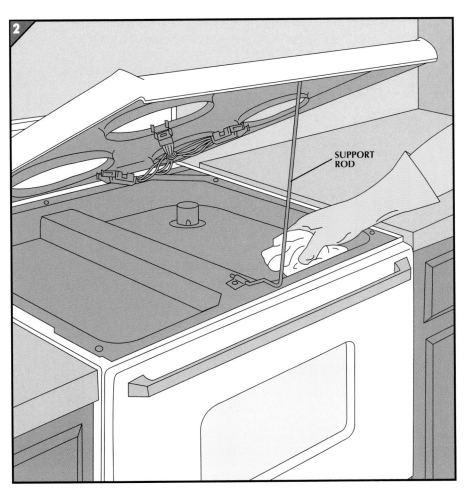

SUPPORT ROD

2. Getting under the top.
◆ Lift the front edge of the cooktop and prop it up with the hinged support rod or a board.
◆ With a vacuum-cleaner crevice attachment, clean up crumbs and dust from under the cooktop.
◆ Wipe the interior with a detergent solution *(left)*. To loosen baked-on spots, scrub with a nylon scouring pad dampened with a heavy-duty degreaser.
◆ Rinse off the cleaner with a damp sponge.

3. Removing the door.

For better access to the oven, remove the door from its hinges.

◆ Open the door and remove any screws securing it to the hinges.

◆ Hold the door partially open and pull it off its hinges *(right)*.

Some oven doors have latched hinges that can be locked in an open position; this feature prevents the hinges from snapping back against the doorframe while the door is being removed. To remove this type of door, open it all the way, lock the latches, and pull the door straight outward, off its hinges.

HINGE

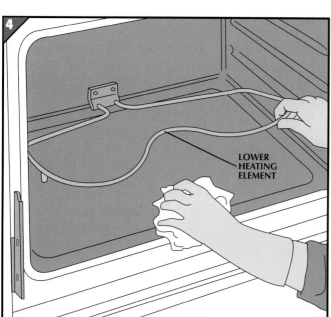

LOWER HEATING ELEMENT

4. Cleaning the oven.

◆ Remove the oven racks and wash them separately.

◆ Wash the oven interior and the inside of the door with detergent or heavy-duty degreaser, then rinse off the cleaner. For a standard oven, you can also use oven cleaner—following the directions and precautions on the label—but do not use it on a continuous-clean type. A self-cleaning oven should not be washed.

◆ To clean the floor of the oven, gently lift up the lower heating element *(left)*; do not try to move the upper element.

◆ Remove the storage drawer under the oven floor by pulling it out and then lifting the front of the drawer to disengage the rollers.

◆ Sponge out the interior of the drawer with a detergent solution, and vacuum or wash the kitchen floor underneath.

TRICKS OF THE TRADE

Steaming a Microwave Clean

Usually, just wiping the interior of a microwave oven after every use will keep it sparkling. But if food spatters have hardened, they may be difficult to remove. Place a large bowl of water in the oven and heat it to boiling. The steam will soften the deposits so you can sponge them away.

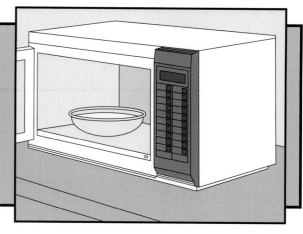

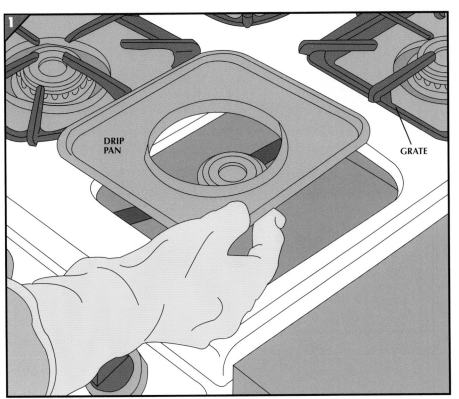

1. Washing grates and drip pans.
◆ If the stove has electrical accessories, unplug it or shut off the power at the service panel.
◆ Lift off the grates. If the drip pans are removable, lift them out as well (left).
◆ Wipe the drip pans clean with a detergent solution; for tough spots, put on rubber gloves and use a white nylon scouring pad and heavy-duty degreaser. Remove baked-on grime from the grates with #1/0 steel wool.
◆ Rinse off any degreaser with water.

2. Cleaning under the cooktop.
◆ Propping the cooktop open with the support rod or by hand, vacuum crumbs and dust from the interior with a crevice tool (right). Try not to jostle pipes and wires.
◆ Sponge the surface with detergent or a heavy-duty degreaser and water; for stubborn spots, scrub them with a nylon scouring pad or steel wool.
◆ Rinse the surface well and dry it with an absorbent cloth.
◆ If the burners are removable, take them out for cleaning, removing any screws holding them in place. If the burners are nonremovable, clean them in place (page 70).
◆ If the stove has pilot lights, make sure they are lit before you lower the top back into position.

3. Cleaning the burners.

◆ Wipe the top ring and the base of the burner with an absorbent cloth moistened with a detergent solution; for burned-on residue, scrub it with a heavy-duty degreaser.

◆ Rinse the burner parts with a damp sponge.

◆ Gently clean each flame opening with a thin wire or pin *(right)*. Do not use a toothpick—it can break off in the hole.

Newer gas ranges may have sealed burners with no holes around them. To clean these, lift off the burner cap *(inset)* and wash it in the sink. Carefully wipe the burner base with a damp cloth.

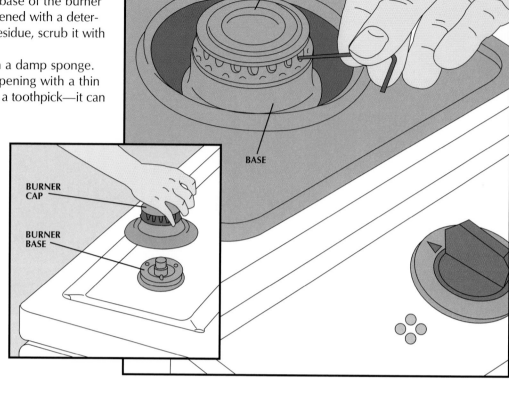

4. Scrubbing down the oven.

◆ Remove the oven door *(page 68, Step 3)* and take out the oven racks. Wash them with detergent and warm water; for burned-on grime, use a heavy-duty degreaser or steel wool.

◆ If the oven has a removable floor, release any latches securing it and take the floor out for cleaning *(right)*.

◆ Scrub the remaining interior surfaces, including the door. If you have removed the oven floor, vacuum but do not scrub beneath it.

◆ Remove the storage drawer or broiler oven for cleaning *(page 68, Step 4)*. (Some broiler drawers have a special latch that releases the drawer for removal.) Then direct your attention to the kitchen floor underneath.

◆ Rinse any surfaces cleaned with a degreaser with water.

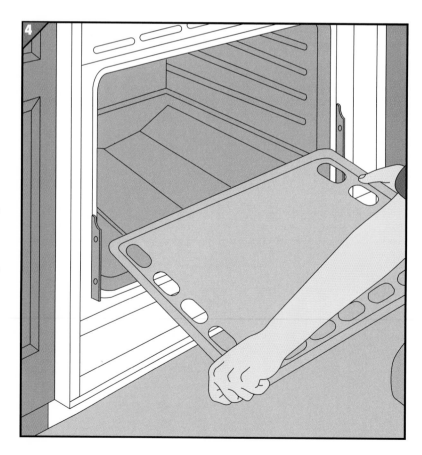

EMPTYING THE LINT TRAP IN A CLOTHES WASHER

Removing and cleaning the trap.
Lint traps can be located in a variety of places; three common types are illustrated here. For those located at the center of the agitator, pull the trap out *(right)* to remove the lint. For a basket trap that fits over the agitator shaft *(inset, left)*, pluck out the lint. A card trap *(inset, right)* slides into a slot in the upper rim of the washer tub; remove it and dislodge the lint by tapping the trap sharply against a solid surface covered with a paper towel.

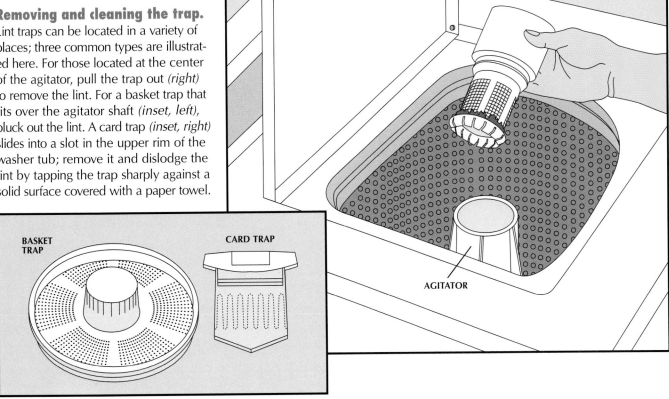

BASKET TRAP

CARD TRAP

AGITATOR

MAINTAINING AIRFLOW THROUGH A DRYER

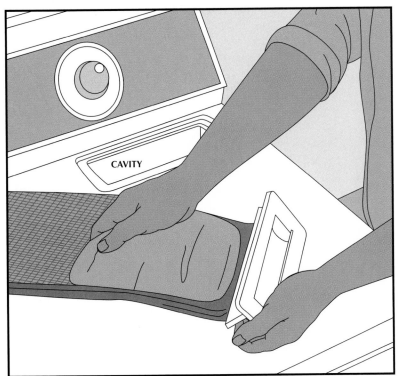

CAVITY

Cleaning a top lint trap.
◆ Pull the lint trap out of its cavity in the top of the dryer.
◆ Gently peel any lint off the screen *(left)*; do not wash the screen.

71

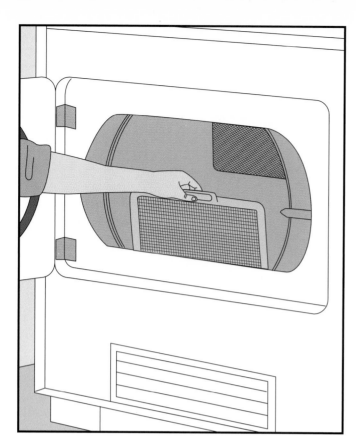

Cleaning a drum trap.
◆ Lift the trap out of its cavity in the dryer opening *(left)*.
◆ Pull lint off the screen; do not wash the screen.

Some older models have a round screened lint trap located in the back of the drum. Pull out the trap and remove the screen, then peel off the lint.

Clearing the air channel.
◆ Loosen the clamp to disconnect the hose from the exhaust vent and brush debris from the opening *(right)*.
◆ Brush or vacuum lint from inside the hose; for a very long hose, you may have to clean it in increments, compressing sections as you work. If there is a pipe rather than a hose, separate the pipe into sections and treat each one individually.
◆ Outdoors, check the flap covering the exhaust vent; if it is damaged or missing, replace it.

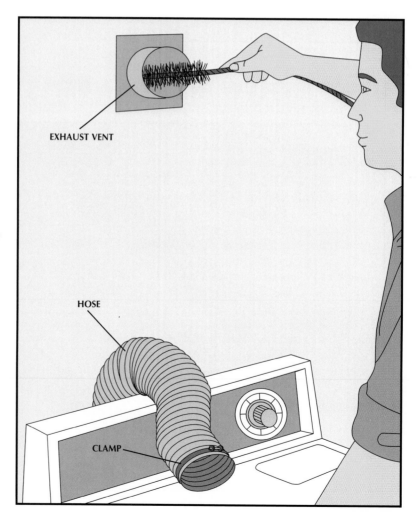

EXHAUST VENT

HOSE

CLAMP

Removing debris.

◆ If the trash compactor's drawer is removable, pull the drawer out as far as it will go; then depress the roller latches on each side *(right)* and pull the drawer to disengage the bottom rollers from the runners.

◆ Wearing work gloves and watching for glass shards, wash the drawer interior with detergent and warm water, then rinse and dry it.

◆ Vacuum and wash the inside walls of the compactor body and wipe the bottom surface of the plunger.

If the compactor drawer is not removable, pull it out as far as you can, then wash and rinse it. Clean the inside of the body by reaching over the top of the opened drawer with a long-handled brush or vacuum cleaner attachment.

LATCH

RUNNER

TRICKS OF THE TRADE

Banishing Garbage-Disposer Odors

Running plenty of water through a garbage disposer while it is operating helps prevent unpleasant smells from developing. If you do notice an odor, you can eliminate it by pouring a handful of ice cubes or citrus peels with some baking powder down the disposer while it is running. Or, pour in a commercial sanitizing product.

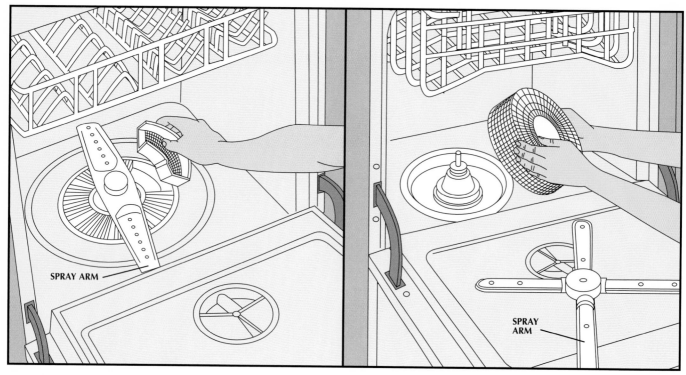

SPRAY ARM

SPRAY ARM

Emptying the filter.

Unless your dishwasher has a self-cleaning filter, empty the filter whenever it collects food particles, stray silverware, or other articles.

◆ To remove a crescent-shaped filter—located beside the spray-arm shaft—press the tab on the side and lift the filter *(above, left)*. Rinse it under running water.

◆ For a round-basket filter seated on the spray arm shaft, pull the spray arm straight up off its shaft, then lift off the filter *(above, right)*. Hold it under running water and scrub it with a brush to dislodge trapped debris.

TRICKS OF THE TRADE

Dealing with Hard-Water Buildup

Over time, mineral deposits from hard water can accumulate inside a dishwasher. To dissolve this buildup, load the racks with clean dishes—do not include any metal items—and set a bowl holding 2 cups of white vinegar in the bottom rack. Do not add detergent, and run the machine through a normal cycle. Treat the dishwasher in this manner only twice a year, as excessive amounts of vinegar can harm the interior surfaces.

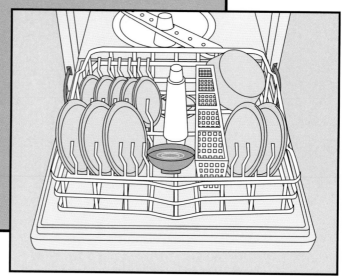

Dust, pollen, smoke, and other airborne pollutants in a home can cause discomfort, trigger allergic reactions, and damage household goods. Airborne cooking grease that builds up in vent fans and ductwork is also a fire hazard.

Impurities are screened out by the filters in range hoods, air conditioners, and furnaces—provided the filters are cleaned periodically or replaced when necessary.

Maintaining Filters: The grease filter on a kitchen exhaust fan is located on the underside of the range hood; clean it once a month *(below)*. Models that recirculate air without venting it to the outdoors also have a charcoal filter stacked on top; replace this filter every three to six months.

Room air conditioners have filters behind the air-intake grille on the front. Wash the filter every two to three weeks *(page 76)*.

On central heating and cooling systems, the filter is positioned between the return-air duct and the blower motor. Inspect the filter once a month when the furnace is in use and replace the filter when necessary *(page 77)*.

Clean electronic air cleaners that hook into a heating and cooling system once a month or when the warning light comes on or the meter so indicates *(pages 77-78)*.

TOOLS

Scrub brush
Screwdriver
Vacuum cleaner
Cotton cloths
Washtub

SERVICING A RANGE HOOD

Pulling out the filter.
◆ For a flat filter, grasp the tab on its edge, then pull the filter out and down to slide it from its channels *(right)*. For an angled filter, release the two latches on one side.
◆ Wash the filter in a solution of mild detergent and water, or clean it in the dishwasher. For a heavy grease buildup, put on rubber gloves and goggles and apply ammonia with a scrub brush, taking care not to disturb the weave of the mesh.
◆ Rinse the piece well and shake it dry before repositioning it.

CARING FOR ROOM AIR CONDITIONERS

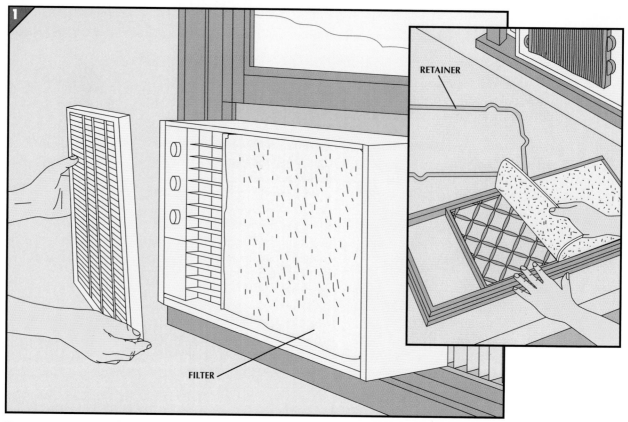

1. Accessing the filter.
◆ Unplug the air conditioner.
◆ Remove any screws holding the front panel in place and pull the panel straight off *(above)*.
◆ Undo any retaining clips holding the filter in place and pull it out. If the filter is held inside the front panel with a wire retainer, disengage the retainer and lift off the filter *(inset)*.

In some models, you can slide the filter out from the top without removing the front panel.

2. Washing the filter.
◆ Vacuum or brush dust off the filter.
◆ Wash the filter in a solution of mild detergent and water. Rinse it with plain water *(right)* and wring it dry. If the filter is damaged or cannot be cleaned, replace it.
◆ With a moist cloth or stiff-bristle brush, clean dust off the inside of the front panel. Wash the panel with a general-purpose detergent; rinse and dry it.
◆ Reinstall the filter in the air conditioner unit.

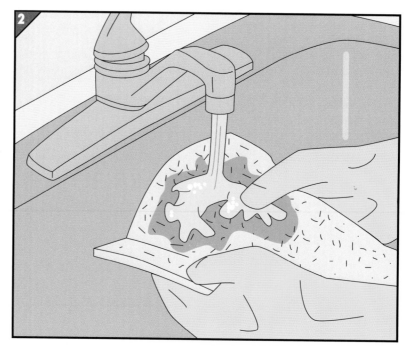

TENDING TO THE FURNACE

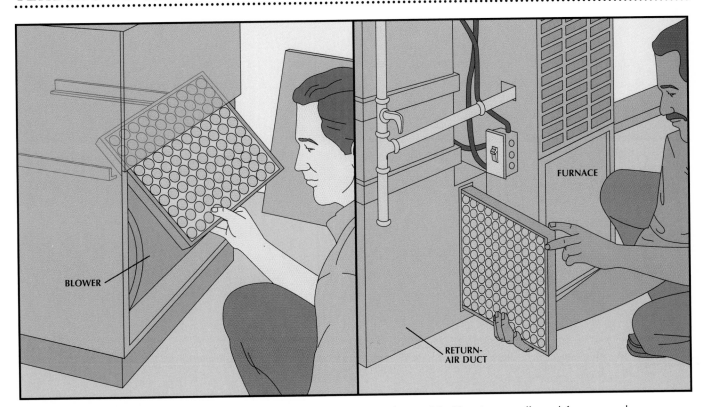

BLOWER

FURNACE

RETURN-AIR DUCT

Removing the filters.
◆ Turn off the power switch for the blower and cut the power to the furnace.
◆ On older furnaces, the air filter may be located behind a removable panel on metal channels above the blower *(above, left)*. On modern systems, the air filter is usually located in a slot between the return-air duct and the furnace *(above, right)*. Remove the filter.

◆ A disposable filter in a cardboard frame, as shown above, that is heavily soiled and matted with dirt, should be replaced with a matching unit. For filters made of a sheet of fiberglass material clipped to a metal frame, you can purchase the material in a roll; remove the old material and clip on a new sheet. Permanent aluminum filters can be washed, but they then need to be recoated with a special oil—leave this type to a professional.

SERVICING ELECTRONIC FILTERS

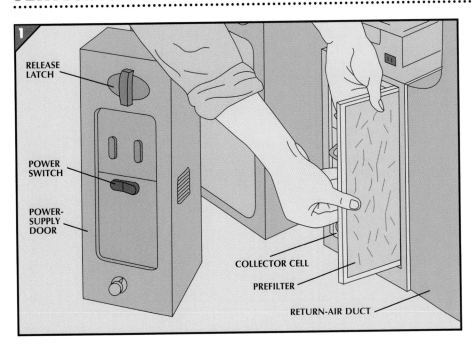

RELEASE LATCH

POWER SWITCH

POWER-SUPPLY DOOR

COLLECTOR CELL

PREFILTER

RETURN-AIR DUCT

1. Taking out the prefilter.
◆ Turn off the power switch on the cleaner's power-supply door; if there is no switch on the door, turn off the furnace blower. Cut the power to the furnace at the service panel.
◆ Disengage the power-supply door by turning its release latch; if there is no latch, simply pull the door straight out.
◆ Slide out the aluminum prefilter, which fits between the collector cell and the return-air duct *(left)*.

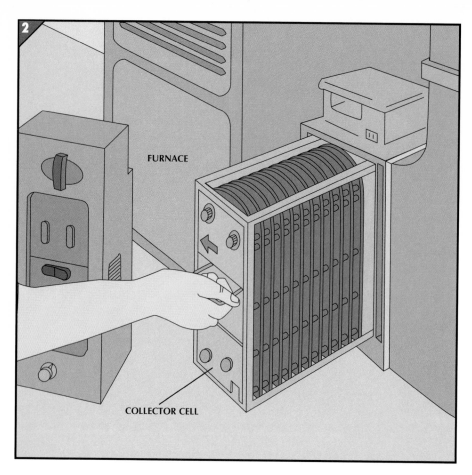

FURNACE

COLLECTOR CELL

2. Removing the cell.

◆ Grasp the handle of the collector cell and slide it out *(left)*.

◆ If there is a second cell placed end to end against the first, remove it as well.

3. Washing the cell and prefilter.

◆ Place the collector cell in a plastic washtub or a bathtub filled with enough water to cover the cell.

◆ Add $\frac{1}{2}$ cup of automatic-dishwasher detergent for every 5 gallons of water, and soak the collector cell for 20 minutes; wearing rubber gloves, agitate it occasionally to loosen the dirt *(right)*.

◆ Remove the cell and swish the prefilter clean in the solution.

◆ In a tub of clear water or with a hose, rinse the cell and prefilter.

◆ When the cell and prefilter are dry, reposition them in the air-cleaner cabinet so the cell handle faces out and the airflow direction arrow points toward the furnace. Put the door back into place and turn on the power switch; you may notice some snapping noises until the cell dries completely.

Clean swimming-pool water is essential to the safety and health of bathers. In addition to performing periodic cleaning and maintenance on a pool, you may occasionally have to take quick action to remedy specific water-quality problems *(pages 122-123)*.

Caring for the Filter System: Clean your pool's strainers and filter about once a week. Depending on the filtering medium—which may be sand, diatomaceous earth (DE), or a cartridge—filters are cleaned either by backwashing them or hosing them down *(pages 82-83)*. To determine when the filter needs cleaning, note the reading on the tank pressure gauge immediately after cleaning the filter; clean it again when the reading has increased by 10 pounds per square inch (psi).

Dealing with Dirt and Debris: Even with efficient filters, some dirt will settle on the sides and bottom of the pool—scoop up large debris from the pool bottom and then vacuum up finer dust and dirt *(page 81)*. Sponge off the grime along the water line with a nonabrasive cleaner designed for pools.

Maintaining the Chemical Balance: Pool water needs just enough disinfectant to kill bacteria and microscopic organisms. Both chlorine and non-chlorine sanitizing systems are available. Adjust the water's pH level—a measure of acidity and alkalinity—so the pool walls and hardware will not corrode or form scale, and minerals will not precipitate out. Pool-supply stores will test a sample of your water when you first fill the pool and advise you on what chemicals to add to establish the appropriate chemical balance.

When the pool is in use, test the chlorine content and pH level every day, and add any necessary chemicals *(page 80)*; test them every other day when the pool is not in use.

Spring Cleaning: To prepare a pool for the bathing season, scrub and vacuum its surfaces, and run the filter system continuously for five days; use a special pool-cleaning brush for scrubbing. Check the pressure reading hourly if the water is very dirty, and clean the filter if it begins to clog.

If the walls of a concrete pool are extremely dirty, drain the pool and scrub it down *(page 83)*. Never drain a vinyl or fiberglass pool to clean it, however—the weight of the water is needed to keep the membrane in place; instead, scrub the walls with a pool-cleaning brush on a telescoping pole.

POOL-CHEMICAL SAFETY

Pool chemicals are highly concentrated—treat them with care and observe the following guidelines when using them:

✔ Follow label instructions and precautions and wear the recommended safety gear.

✔ Never mix pool chemicals. When using more than one in sequence, allow an hour between treatments. Keep a separate measuring device for each chemical, and keep the device dry.

✔ Store chemicals in a cool, dry place in their original containers, off the ground and out of reach of children. Always keep containers covered, and do not reuse an empty container—rinse it well, then discard it.

✔ Do not smoke while handling pool chemicals. Never leave combustible materials, such as a paper cup, in or near chemical containers.

✔ Avoid touching or inhaling any chemical. Wash your hands after using them. Hose down any area where chemicals have spilled.

 TOOLS

Pool test kit
Pool leaf rake
Pool vacuum
Submersible pump
Screwdriver
Plastic pail
Sponge
Plastic watering can
Pool-cleaning brush
Acid-wash brush

CHECKING THE CHEMICAL BALANCE

Using a pool test kit.
◆ Fill the chlorine vial with pool water taken from 18 inches below the surface, away from inlets.
◆ Add the amount of chlorine reagent indicated in the instructions.
◆ Put the cap on the vial, shake it for a few seconds, and compare the color with the color chart printed on the vial. Note the chlorine level, measured in parts per million (ppm).
◆ Test the pH similarly: To the water in the pH vial, add chlorine neutralizer and phenol red. Cap the vial, shake it, then compare the color to the chart on the vial. Note the corresponding pH reading.
◆ Add chlorine to the pool if the chlorine test registered less than 0.4 ppm.
◆ Correct the pH level if the test does not produce a reading between 7.4 and 7.6.
◆ Rinse the vials well with pool water.

Do not use test chemicals more than 6 months old—they will give inaccurate results.

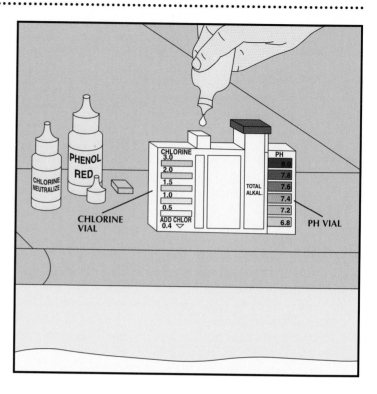

HOW A POOL REFRESHES ITSELF

A pool filter system.
The water in this pool is pumped through the filter tank—water at the bottom of the pool is drawn through the main drain; surface water is sucked through a skimmer opening at the rim. The water goes through the pump and into the filter tank, where a filter medium traps suspended dirt; the water returns to the pool through inlets in the wall. Larger debris, such as leaves and twigs, are trapped in a basket at the base of the skimmer (inset, left). Finer pieces, such as hair and lint, are filtered out by a strainer basket at the pump (inset, right). Remove and empty both baskets about once a week, and clean them with a hose.

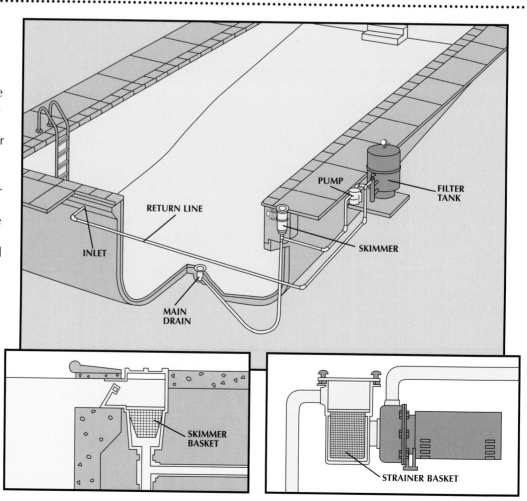

Scooping up debris.

To gather waterlogged leaves and other debris on the bottom of a pool, rest the metal frame of a long-handled net—called a leaf rake—on the pool bottom and pull the rake toward you, trapping the debris in the net *(left)*. Scoop up floating objects by dipping the rake beneath the items.

A jet vacuum—sometimes called a leaf gobbler *(photograph)*—can also be used to pick up large debris. Attach a mesh collector bag to the plastic base of the tool, a garden hose to the coupling on the vacuum plate, and a long pool pole to the bracket provided. Connect the other end of the hose to a faucet. Turn on the water full force, and lower the vacuum to the bottom of the pool. Push it slowly along the bottom, filling the collector bag. This model has a brush on the bottom designed for vinyl pools; models for concrete pools roll on wheels.

Vacuuming a pool.

◆ Attach the special vacuum hose and a long pool pole to the vacuum head.
◆ Slowly submerge the vacuum head until it rests on the pool bottom, then let the rest of the hose fill completely with pool water.
◆ Fit the hose into the suction outlet in the skimmer or to the separate vacuum outlet in the pool wall, if your pool has one. Then switch the filter system to the vacuum setting.
◆ Beginning at the center of the pool, guide the head across the bottom and up the sides to the water line *(right)*. Then reverse direction, pushing the head back to the center of the pool. Repeat this action, moving around the pool's walls.

Automatic vacuum systems for pools make the job even easier. The type shown in the photograph attaches to the pool vacuum outlet. The ensuing water pressure allows the tool to propel itself forward along the bottom of the pool as it sucks up dirt.

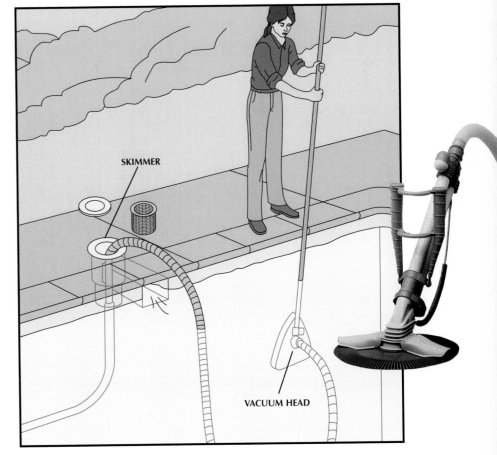

SKIMMER

VACUUM HEAD

Backwashing a sand filter.

◆ Turn off the pool-water heater, then turn off the pump and empty the pump strainer basket.

◆ If the pump has a rotary valve, turn the valve handle to the backwash position *(left)*. If the system has a cylindrical valve, pull up the plunger handle.

◆ Start the pump and monitor the waste water in the sight glass. (If the filter has no sight glass, monitor the appearance of the waste water as it drains away.) When the water runs clear—usually within three to five minutes—stop the pump.

◆ If the valve has a rinse setting, turn the handle to this position and run the pump for 45 seconds to flush out any residue.

◆ Return the valve to its normal position and turn on the pump.

Servicing a DE system.

◆ Turn off the pool-water heater, then turn off the pump and clean the strainer basket.

◆ If the filter has a separation tank, open its shutoff valve; otherwise, open its drain.

◆ If the filter has a cylindrical valve, pull up the plunger handle *(right)*. If the filter has a rotary valve, turn the valve to the backwash setting.

◆ Start the pump and monitor the appearance of the waste water—in a sight glass, if there is one, or at the drain.

◆ When the waste water runs clear, shut off the pump.

◆ Clean the separation tank: First shut off the pump, open the air-relief valve, and remove the drain cap. Open the tank, remove the strainer bag and dispose of its contents. Hose off the bag, return it to the tank, and close the tank. Close the valve and replace the cap, then turn on the pump.

◆ Return the water-flow valve to its normal position for filtering; if there is a separation tank, close the valve to it.

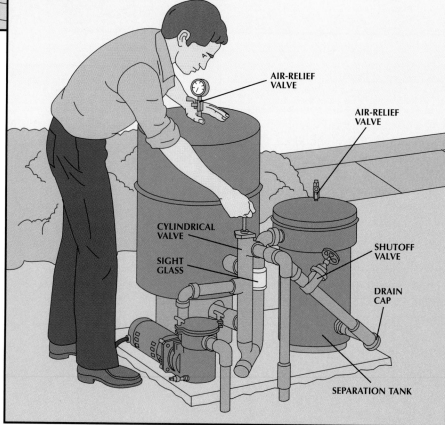

To replenish the diatomaceous earth, turn on the pump and clear the filter of air by opening its air-relief valve. When water trickles from the valve, close it.

Mix a thin slurry of diatomaceous earth and water—using the amounts listed on the system's specification plate—and pour it into the pool skimmer opening.

Hosing down a cartridge filter.
◆ Turn off the pump and the pool-water heater, if there is one. Clean the strainer basket.
◆ Close any valves leading to or from the filter tank. Open the tank air-relief valve, if there is one.
◆ Unlock the tank lid and lift out the cartridge element.
◆ With a garden hose, rinse off the cartridge elements *(left)*. Replace any with holes or tears.
◆ If water fails to remove the dirt, soak each cartridge in filter-cleaning solution, available from pool-supply stores. If this treatment fails, install new cartridges.
◆ Return the cartridge element to the tank, replace the lid, and lock it securely. Open any valves to the filter tank and turn on the pump. When water begins to trickle from the air-relief valve, close it.

SCRUBBING CONCRETE WITH ACID

Washing down the walls.
◆ Turn off electrical power to the pool, then drain it with a submersible pump.
◆ Hose off loose dirt from the pool walls, driving it toward the main drain, and pump out this water. With a cup and a sponge, remove any water remaining in the skimmer.

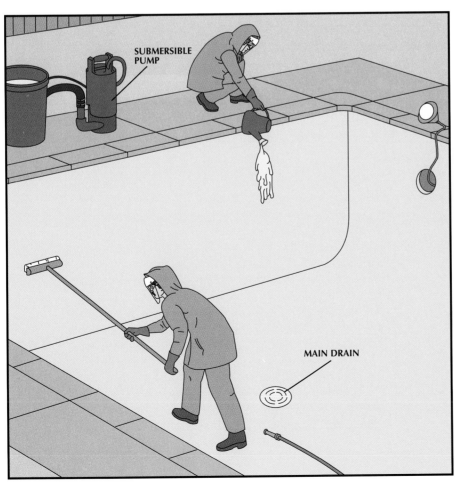

◆ Unscrew the covers of underwater lighting fixtures, remove the fixtures from their niches, then flush out the niches with the hose.
◆ Wearing goggles, rubber rain gear, nitrile gloves, rubber boots, and a face shield, mix a four-to-one solution of muriatic acid in a large plastic trash can. Pour the solution down the walls of the pool from a large plastic watering can.
◆ Have a similarly attired helper scrub the pool in sections with a special pool broom designed for use with acid *(left)*.
◆ Hose off each section after scrubbing it, pushing the waste water toward the main drain.
◆ When the entire pool has been scrubbed, run the submersible pump to remove the waste water around the main drain.
◆ Flush the trash can and watering can with fresh water.
◆ To clean acid from the main drain and the submersible pump, remove the drain cover, set the pump in the drain, flood the area with fresh water, and pump the water out.

⚠️ **CAUTION** *Always pour acid into water, not the reverse, and avoid splashing it.*

Dealing with the Aftermath of a Flood

After a flood, it is essential that you dry out the house and its contents as quickly as possible. Immediate action can reduce damage and cleanup costs by preventing mildew and fungus growth and pervasive, lingering odors. Although the first task is to turn off the electricity (*opposite*), your approach to cleaning up depends on whether you are dealing with clean water—such as from a plumbing leak—or dirty water—such as from a flood or sewer—which can contaminate the house.

Getting Rid of the Water: Drain a waterlogged ceiling as soon as possible to prevent it from collapsing. Then turn to removing standing water. An upper floor will drain by itself. You can remove up to 2 inches of water from a basement with a wet/dry vacuum, but to drain out more water than this, rent a gas-powered trash pump (*page 86*). Open wall cavities to drain water from between walls (*pages 87-88*). If the water is clean and the wall is uninsulated, let the wallboard or plaster dry in place. When the water is dirty or there is insulation in place, remove the wallboard or plaster and insulation (*pages 89-90*), and put up new insulation and wallboard once the wall cavities are dry.

Cleaning and Drying: Rinse off the walls and floor and the duct work, if you can access it. The process of drying the house can be speeded up with proper ventilation (*page 90*). If doors and windows must be kept closed, use a dehumidifier to take excess moisture from the air. Consider renting a portable propane heater equipped with a blower to help dry the rooms. To avoid carbon monoxide poisoning, provide adequate ventilation by keeping windows open in the room. Do not operate this type of heater while the house is occupied, but check on it frequently.

Finally, clean, sanitize, and dry the contents of the house (*page 91*). Items contaminated by dirty floodwater will have to be discarded.

> ⚠ **CAUTION** *After an environmental disaster, do not go back to your house until permission is given by local authorities. At the house, be alert for downed power lines, foundation cracks, damage to roofs and overhangs, stairs that have separated from the house, ceilings that may collapse, or furniture that may topple; and do not enter if you have any doubts that it is safe to do so. If you suspect a gas leak, leave immediately and call your utility.*

TOOLS

Mop	Mop
Sponges	Shovel
Wet/dry vacuum	Hammer
Broom	Utility knife
Trash pump	Putty knife
Ice pick	Pry bar
Long-handled squeegee	Stud sensor
	Wood chisel
	Compass saw

SAFETY TIPS

Wear rubber gloves and an antibacterial mask when cleaning up from dirty or contaminated floodwater; add goggles when demolishing a wall or draining a ceiling.

> ⚠ **CAUTION**
>
> ## Water and Wiring: A Hazardous Combination
>
> *Any time house wiring and water come together, there is a danger of electric shock. Before you allow family members into a house that has been flooded, turn off the power—either by shutting it off at the service panel, or by having an electrician disconnect it. When entering the house, do not try to turn on lights or plug in a work light—carry a flashlight to illuminate your way. If the service panel is in a room with submerged electrical receptacles, do not enter the room or attempt to disarm the panel—call in an electrician. When there is moisture on or near the panel or standing water in the room, wear tall, leak-free rubber boots and stand on a dry wooden ladder or stool while working. Once the power is off, have an electrician assess the damage and make any necessary repairs or reconnect an undamaged circuit or two to provide temporary power for drying the house.*

Shutting down a circuit-breaker panel.
Following all the safety precautions opposite and wearing dry rubber gloves, use a dry wooden or plastic stick to flip off the main breaker switch located at the top of the panel *(left)*.

Disarming a fuse box.
Following all the precautions opposite and wearing dry rubber gloves, insert a dry wooden or plastic stick between the handle and the front of the fuse block. With a hand at either end of the stick, pull out the block *(right)*.

Instead of a main fuse block, some older fuse boxes have a cutoff lever mounted at the top of one side of the box. To cut the power, push the lever to the off position with a dry stick.

DRAINING A CEILING

Punching holes.

◆ To drain a ceiling sagging under the weight of water, first center a leakproof trash can under the bulge.

◆ Drive a finishing nail into the end of a broom handle and, standing away from the sag, start at the edge of the bulge and punch a hole in the ceiling *(right)*. Be prepared to step back quickly in case part of the ceiling material falls.

◆ Work toward the center to poke a series of drainage holes in the bulge.

◆ If the water was dirty, remove the wallboard. Where there is insulation, remove the wallboard and insulation.

For a damp spot that is not bulging, place a bucket under the wet area and, standing on a ladder, poke a hole in the ceiling at the center of the spot with an ice pick or a nail.

GETTING RID OF STANDING WATER

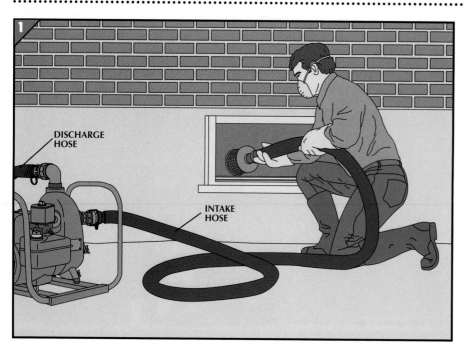

DISCHARGE HOSE

INTAKE HOSE

1. Pumping out a basement.

◆ Set up a trash pump and position the discharge hose over a storm drain.

◆ Start the pump and feed the intake hose through a basement window *(left)*, lowering the hose until the strainer is submerged in the water.

◆ Pump out 2 to 3 feet of water and mark the water level on a wall.

◆ The next day, check whether the water level has risen. If so, wait another couple of days before continuing to pump. Otherwise, pump out another 2 to 3 feet per day, continuing until the strainer will no longer pick up water.

⚠ *Do not pump out more than 3 feet of water per day;*
CAUTION *removing more can cause walls to buckle or cave in.*

2. Shoveling out debris.

◆ In the basement, push mud and debris to the center of the room with a long-handled squeegee, then shovel it into a large trash can.

◆ On upper floors, place a trash can under a window. If there are garden beds below, construct a trough from two 1-by-12s nailed together in an L shape. If the trough will be longer than 12 feet, use 2-by-12s.

◆ Shovel the debris out the window or into the trough *(left)*.

◆ Flush the floors and walls with clean water and disinfectant. Sop up any remaining moisture with a sponge or a mop.

TRICKS OF THE TRADE

Improvising a Squeegee

Rather than buying a squeegee, you can construct one from two ordinary yard implements—a rake and an old hose. Cut a short length of garden hose and make a slit down its length, then fit the hose over the tines of the rake.

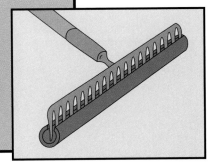

DRAINING WALLS

1. Removing shoe molding.

◆ Run a utility knife along the top of the shoe molding to break any paint seal.

◆ At one end of the wall, insert the blade of a putty knife behind the molding. Tap it gently to open a gap behind the molding *(right)*.

◆ Protecting the baseboard with a piece of scrap wood, slip a pry bar into the gap. Gently pry the molding away from the baseboard, working your way along the wall.

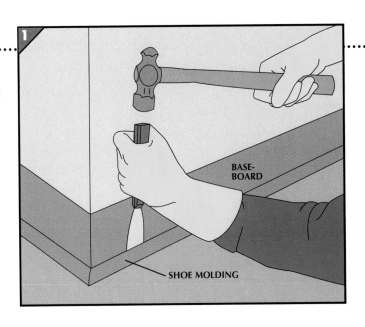

BASE-BOARD

SHOE MOLDING

2. Prying off baseboards.

◆ Hammer the curved end of a pry bar between the top of the baseboard and the wall *(left)*.

◆ Wedge a plywood scrap behind the pry bar to protect the wall *(inset)* and open a gap of about 1 inch between the baseboard and the wall.

◆ Release the bar to allow the baseboard to spring back toward the wall, leaving the nail heads slightly exposed.

◆ Pull out the nails with the claw end of the bar, protecting the baseboard with a piece of wood.

◆ Repeat at 2-foot intervals along the wall until the entire baseboard is free.

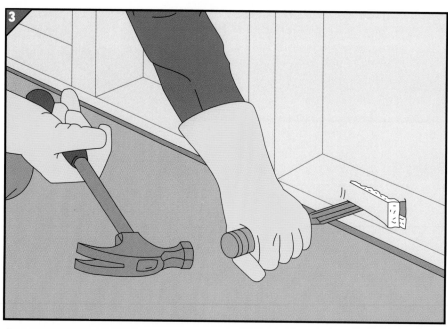

3. Piercing the wall.

◆ Locate two consecutive wall studs with a stud sensor or by tapping along the wall with a hammer—it will sound hollow between studs.

◆ With a hammer and a wood chisel, cut a 1-by-3-inch opening through the drywall or plaster about 1 inch above the floor, centered between the wall studs *(above)*.

◆ Open a similar hole directly above the first a few inches below the ceiling.

◆ Repeat between every pair of studs along the length of the wall.

REMOVING WET WALL MATERIAL

1. Breaking wallboard.
◆ Remove the shoe molding and baseboard *(pages 87-88)*.
◆ For wallboard, score the wall 4 feet from the floor with a utility knife.
◆ With a hammer or a pry bar, break holes through the interior wall to a point just above the line left by the floodwater *(right)*.
◆ Where the interior wall is wallboard, reach into the holes and pull the sodden material off the studs, removing nails as necessary to free the wallboard. In a plaster wall, insert a pry bar into the holes and pull away the plaster and lath.

2. Cutting away insulation.
◆ With a board cut to fit between the studs, compress the insulation just below the top of the wall opening. Using the board as a straightedge, slice through the insulation with a utility knife *(left)*, being careful not to cut into any wires.
◆ Pull the wet insulation out of the wall and discard it.
◆ Wash the wall and framing members with disinfectant.

Rigid polystyrene insulation can be left in place and cleaned with disinfectant, then hosed off.

3. Trimming wallboard.

◆ Cut along the scored line with a compass saw *(right)*, being careful not to cut into any wires.

◆ When the wall is completely dry, install new insulation and wallboard.

QUICK-DRYING WITH FRESH AIR

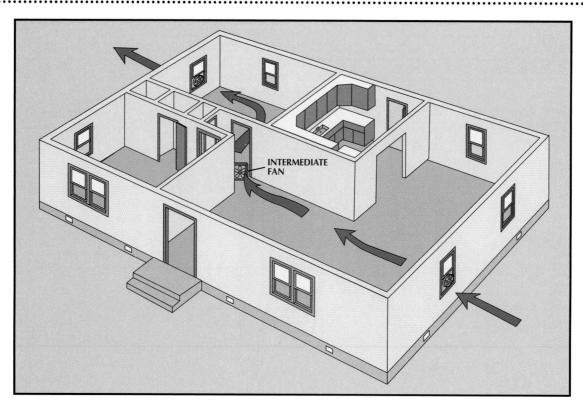

INTERMEDIATE FAN

Moving air through the house.

◆ When the weather is dry, open all the windows and doors of the house.

◆ Place a fan in a window on the windward side of the house. On the opposite end of the house, set up a second fan to exhaust air. If interior walls slow the air current, or if the fans are very far apart, set up intermediate fans as well.

Taking quick action to dry household items can minimize water damage. Clean items before drying them, using disinfectant, if necessary.

Area Rugs: Discard rugs with foam backing. Lay other rugs across a clothesline and direct fans over them.

Carpets: Tear up and discard carpeting that has been soaked with dirty floodwater. If the water was clean, remove all furniture from the carpet and open windows and doors to circulate air. Vacuum out as much water as possible with a wet/dry vacuum. Then speed the drying with fans *(below)*.

Artwork: Entrust valuable art to a professional immediately. If this is not possible, remove wet items from the frame, glass, and backing. (Items that have begun to dry may stick to the glass and should be left in their frames.) Place the art in a cool, dry place, away from sunlight. For canvas paintings, lay pieces face down on a towel. For art on paper, set the item under towel-covered plywood and set a heavy weight on top; remove the plywood occasionally to let air reach the paper. If the towel gets damp, change it for a dry one. Prints and posters that have curled can be placed between two sheets of paper and ironed on a low setting.

Books and Papers: Store valuable books and papers in plastic bags in a freezer until you have an opportunity to dry them. If this isn't possible, seal them in a plastic bag with moth crystals. Dry wet items with a blow-dryer; do not force stuck pages apart. If the pages are only damp, stand the books on end with pages separated for an hour; then stack them and weight them down for an hour. Repeat the process until the pages are dry.

Furniture: If weather permits, dry furniture outdoors out of direct sunlight. Remove drawers and open doors; if they are swollen shut, leave them and, if possible, remove the back of the piece to circulate air. Have a professional clean upholstered furniture soaked with dirty water. Meanwhile, take cushions off and dry them separately.

Bedding and Clothing: If you cannot have down-filled pillows and cushions dry-cleaned immediately, tumble them in the clothes dryer with several terry-cloth towels and a pair of clean sneakers. Dry feather quilts this way or across a clothesline. Reposition and shake them frequently to distribute feathers. Discard waterlogged mattresses. Air-dry or fan-dry damp mattresses. To sanitize clothing, add chlorine bleach to the wash water.

Leather Goods: Dry leather away from direct sunlight and heat.

Metal Fixtures: To protect lock mechanisms, squirt light household oil into the bolt opening and keyhole, and work the lock and knob to distribute the oil. Clean hinges, then oil them. Dry faucets and light fixtures with a towel. Coat them with petroleum jelly to keep humidity from corroding them.

Appliances: Do not use the washing machine or dishwasher until the municipal water supply has been declared potable. Then, run machines once with a solution of hot water and disinfectant.

Kitchen Items: Discard all food items, including canned goods, as well as soft plastic and other porous items that contacted dirty water. Wash dishes in disinfectant.

A POWERFUL FAN FOR DRYING CARPETS

To prevent mildew from forming on carpets, it is essential that they be dried quickly. You can call in a professional, or you can do the job yourself with a special fan *(right)*. For carpet that is tacked down around the edges, pull up a corner and place the mouth of the fan underneath. Glued-down carpeting will have to be dried in place.

91

Controlling Household Pests

Encountering ants, crickets, and cockroaches in your home can be disturbing, to say the least; but when rats and termites invade a house, they endanger lives and property. This chapter identifies some of the most common household pests, and presents effective techniques for keeping them out and evicting or destroying those that find their way in.

Pestproofing a House   94

Pinpointing Trouble Spots
Sealing Off Entry Points

Taking Offensive Action   100

Indoor Tactics
Laying Down a Chemical Barrier
Destroying the Nests of Outdoor Pests
Trapping Mice and Rats

A Guide to Common Pests   105

Sealing a pipe chase →

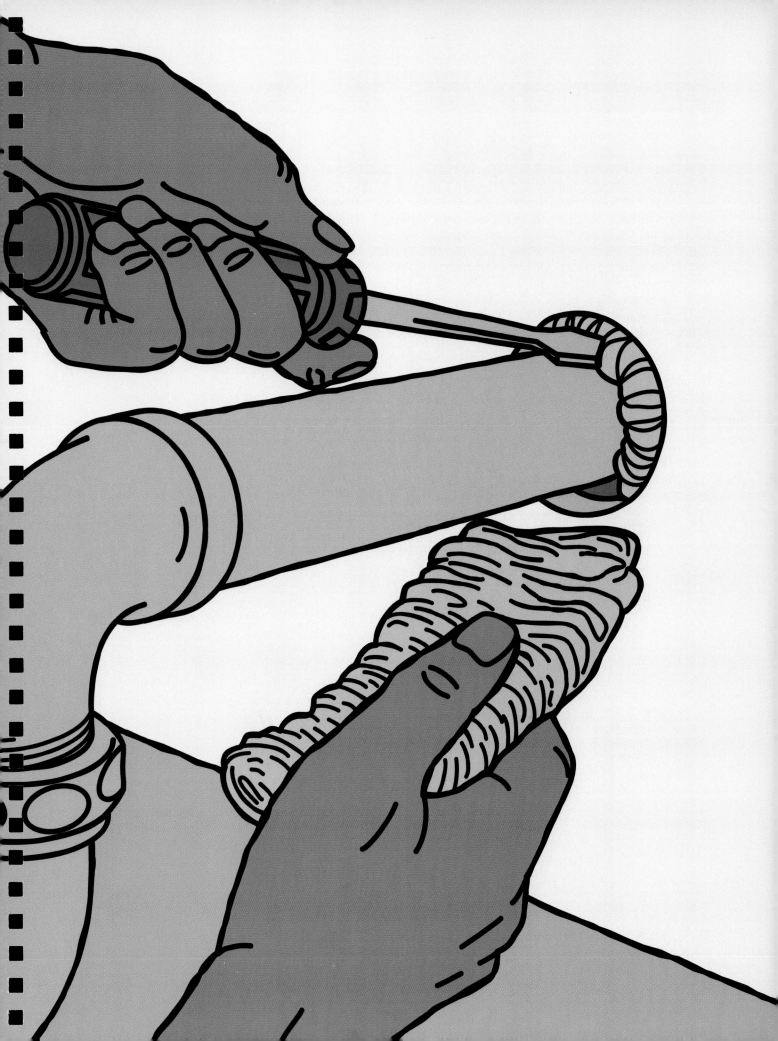

Pestproofing a House

Pests can be merely annoying or downright destructive. Many varieties destroy foodstuffs, clothing, furniture, rugs, and books; termites and carpenter ants can even undermine the structure of a house. The first line of defense, often overlooked, is routine cleaning that reaches into the places where pests nest and feed. The next tactic is to seal off points of entry, hiding places, and travel routes.

Keeping Things Clean: Thorough housecleaning *(below)* will deprive pests of food particles and the pockets of dust in which they hide. Yard cleanup can eliminate conditions that encourage development of large pest populations *(opposite)*.

Blocking Entry Points: Look out for cracks in walls—these are favorite hiding places for pests, as well as passageways for insects traveling into the house from outside. Plugging, caulking, and screening such openings *(pages 96-98)* is often sufficient to prevent a major infestation or cure a minor one. Even if you have to apply a pesticide, blocking entry points will protect your house long after the chemical is no longer effective.

Termites: Ridding a house of termites—and keeping them out—requires special action. Several preventive measures can be built into a house during its construction, while others can be incorporated into an existing structure *(page 99)*.

 TOOLS

Vacuum cleaner	Stiff fiber brush
Caulking gun	Router
Putty knife	Handsaw
Wrench	Wooden mallet
Hand stapler	
Cold chisel	Sanding block
Maul	Screwdriver

 SAFETY TIPS

Protect your eyes with goggles when using a cold chisel or a power tool.

KEEPING PESTS AT BAY

Routine attention to areas where pests shelter and feed is often sufficient to prevent an infestation.

✔ Remove dust and crumbs from cracks and crevices and from dark, damp places. Pay special attention to cracks between floorboards and around countertops, cabinets, and baseboards; the inner corners of cabinets; gaps between loose flooring and tiles; pockets behind loose wallpaper; and pipe chases—the openings through which pipes pass.

✔ Remove kick plates and grilles from the refrigerator and dishwasher, and broiler drawers from stoves to vacuum the floor. Vacuum refrigerator coils and scrub the wall behind the stove to prevent grease buildup. Rinse out the garbage can from time to time, and keep it tightly covered. Clean up spilled pet food and water, and wash food bowls regularly. Repair leaky faucets.

✔ Store unrefrigerated food in tightly sealed containers. Check shopping bags for stray cockroaches when you first come in from the store. Do not allow stacks of paper bags, newspapers, or magazines to accumulate; they are prime hiding places for insects.

✔ Vacuum under furniture and the loose edges of carpets and rugs. Reposition rugs and carpets periodically or rearrange the furniture to reach all areas for cleaning. Use vacuum-cleaner attachments to remove dust from the crevices of upholstered furniture, the folds of drapes, and the fins of radiators and baseboard heaters. Dust around door hinges and picture frames and under wall hangings. Occasionally, remove heating registers and vacuum or wash behind them.

✔ Before storing seasonal clothing, clean it. Close the doors or drawers of the storage units tightly. If they do not close, seal them with masking tape.

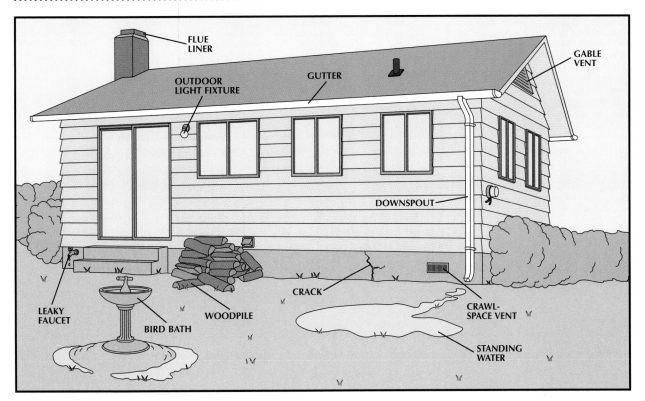

FLUE LINER

OUTDOOR LIGHT FIXTURE

GUTTER

GABLE VENT

DOWNSPOUT

CRACK

CRAWL-SPACE VENT

LEAKY FAUCET

BIRD BATH

WOODPILE

STANDING WATER

Preventing an invasion.

Locate woodpiles, compost heaps, and garbage cans away from the house. Keep garbage in cans with snug lids. Cut grass regularly, and trim shrubbery so it doesn't brush against the house. If your yard has trees, clean gutters at least twice a year. Place splash blocks under downspouts, fix dripping faucets, and fill in depressions where water collects. If necessary, improve drainage to eliminate standing water. Filter or frequently change the water in garden pools and birdbaths so that it does not stagnate. Install yellow insect bulbs in outdoor lighting fixtures.

Fill cracks in the foundation walls *(page 97)* and caulk gaps between the siding and the foundation or around window and door frames *(page 98)*. Repair damaged screens, and install screens behind crawl space and attic vents. If the chimney is uncovered, cap the flue liner *(page 96)*.

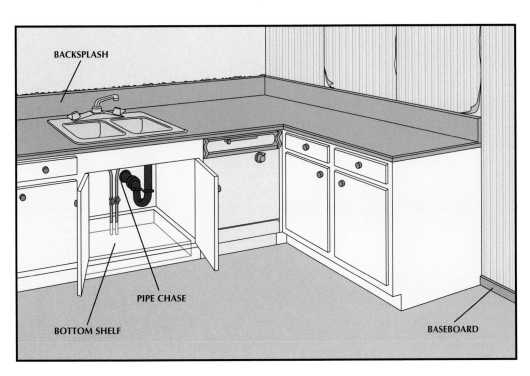

BACKSPLASH

PIPE CHASE

BOTTOM SHELF

BASEBOARD

Eliminating indoor hiding places.

Close any openings that lead into the cavity below the bottom shelf of a cabinet. Fill and seal open pipe chases *(page 98)*, and caulk cracks around countertops, especially behind the backsplash. Reglue loose sections of wallpaper.

Fill crevices around window and door frames with caulk or spackling compound; seal cracks along the bottom of the baseboard with caulk; and patch broken floorboards *(page 97)*.

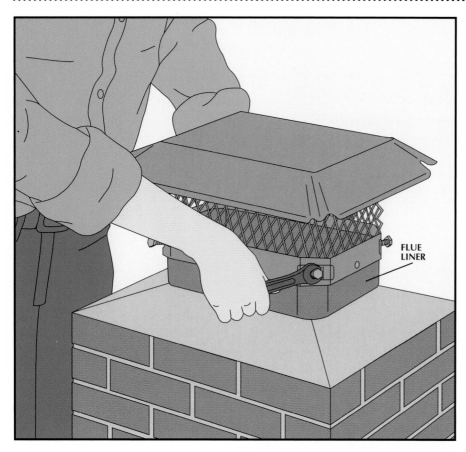

Capping a chimney.
To keep squirrels and birds from getting into your chimney, install a prefabricated chimney cover.
◆ Purchase a cover of the appropriate size and shape for your flue liner.
◆ Fit the base around the flue liner and tighten the bolts against the liner *(left)*.

FLUE LINER

Screening an attic vent.
◆ Cut a piece of window screening large enough to cover the vent with an overlap of at least 1 inch all around.
◆ With a hand stapler, fasten the screening at 1-inch intervals to the frame around the vent *(right)*.

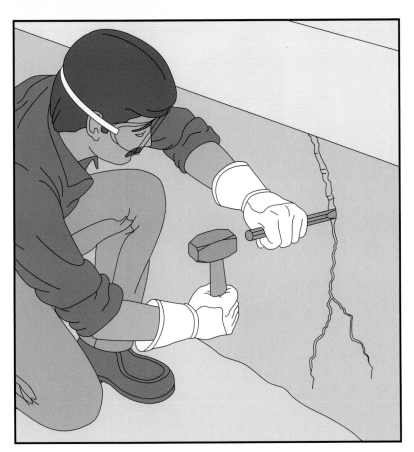

Filling a crack in the foundation.

If the crack is horizontal or its edges are tapered, misaligned, or farther apart than $\frac{1}{8}$ inch, have a building professional inspect it—the crack can point to a serious structural problem.

◆ To repair a crack, use a cold chisel and maul to enlarge it to at least $\frac{1}{4}$ inch wide and $\frac{1}{2}$ inch deep *(left)*.

◆ Clean out loose material with a stiff fiber brush.

◆ Fill the crack with latex concrete-patching compound.

◆ Tape polyethylene sheeting over the patch and let it cure.

Setting in a floor spline.

◆ For a floorboard crack that is wider than $\frac{1}{4}$ inch (a narrower crack need not be filled), use a router with a small-diameter straight bit to make the width of the crack uniform.

◆ Cut a spline—a thin strip of matching wood—to fit snugly in the crack.

◆ Coat the edge of the broken floorboard and the mating side of the spline with wood glue; then tap the spline into place with a wooden mallet *(right)*.

◆ Sand the patch even with the floor and apply a matching finish to the spline *(page 17)*.

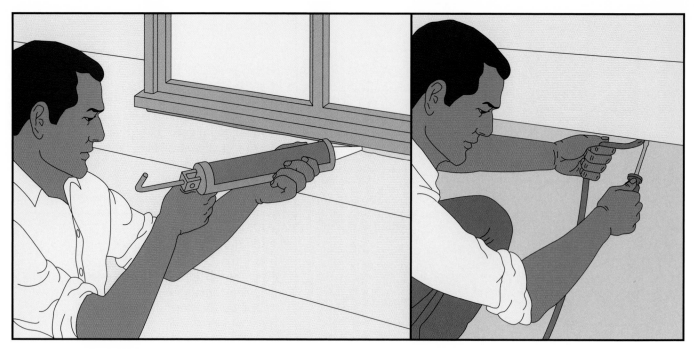

Filling cracks and gaps.

◆ If a crack is narrower than $\frac{1}{4}$ inch, first scrape dirt, old sealant, and flaking paint out of it with a putty knife.

◆ Starting at the far end of the crack, hold a caulking gun at a 45-degree angle to the surface and push the tip of the tube into the crack.

◆ Squeeze the trigger while moving the gun along to inject a continuous bead of caulk into the crack *(above, left)*.

◆ Smooth the caulk with a wet putty knife.

Fill gaps larger than $\frac{1}{4}$ inch with a length of foam backer rod slightly wider than the crack. With a screwdriver, push the rod into the gap so it sits $\frac{1}{4}$ inch below the wall surface *(above, right)*. Then fill the crack to the surface with caulk.

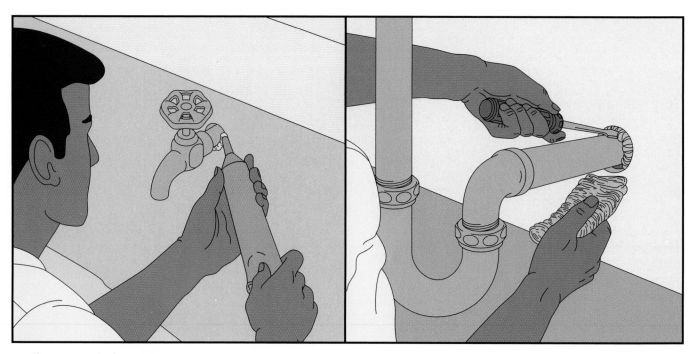

Sealing around pipes and conduits.
Fill gaps up to $\frac{1}{4}$ inch wide around an outdoor faucet, pipe, or conduit with silicone caulk in a roll-up tube. Starting at the bottom of the fixture, apply the sealant by squeezing the tube and moving it upward around the fixture *(above, left)*. Seal gaps wider than $\frac{1}{4}$ inch with foam backer rod and caulk.

To seal a pipe chase under a sink, push wads of steel wool into the gap with a broad-tipped screwdriver *(above, right)*. Fill the space to within $\frac{1}{4}$ inch of the wall surface. Seal the remaining space with silicone caulk.

The most common species of termite lives in damp soil, building mud shelter tubes to travel between soil and wood, and tunneling into wood only to feed. Lumber too close to damp ground is an open invitation to these insects.

When a house is constructed, there are a number of ways it can be made to deter termites. At least 18 inches of space between crawl-space soil and joists, and at least 6 inches between wooden siding and the ground makes the framing less of a temptation. In basements, wood framing that sits on top of a concrete floor, rather than extending into or through it, is essential. A poured-concrete foundation wall, reinforced to resist cracking, has a smoother surface than a concrete-block one, giving termites fewer hiding places for shelter tubes. On a block foundation, a reinforced poured-concrete cap, 4 inches thick, forces the insects to build their tubes across it out in the open, where they are more easily detected; a top course of coreless concrete blocks with tightly filled mortar joints is second best. On a brick-veneer house, 8 inches of concrete foundation wall between the brickwork and the ground will prevent termites from using mortar joints between bricks to travel from soil to wood.

For an existing house, you can also take measures to make the house less vulnerable to termites:

✔ Keep the ground around the foundation and in the crawl space from remaining damp for long periods by correcting poor drainage and improving ventilation. Inspect and repair gutters and downspouts. Regrade the soil if necessary, making sure dirt used for backfill contains no roots, tree limbs, or scrap wood. Encourage airflow through crawl spaces by installing at least one vent for every 200 square feet of floor space. Trim grass and shrubs in front of vents so airflow is not blocked. Clear debris from the crawl space to help dispel dampness, but if moisture persists, cover the floor with plastic sheeting or roofing felt to keep the dampness from permeating the framing above.

✔ Make sure the wood frames of basement windows are at least 6 inches above the soil, adding window wells if necessary.

✔ Construct a concrete base for any wooden steps lacking one, making it at least 6 inches high, and separated from the foundation wall by a minimum of 2 inches (below, right).

✔ On pier-type foundations, ensure that the wood lattice used to screen the openings between piers is at least 2 inches above the ground and separated from the piers by the same amount.

✔ Fill any gaps in the foundation, such as those around pipes and conduits, with sealant.

✔ Use pressure-treated wood for below-grade projects—the chemicals in the wood act as a deterrent to termites.

✔ Once a year, inspect the house foundation for mud shelter tubes.

✔ For extra protection, have an exterminator treat the soil around the foundation with a chemical termite barrier.

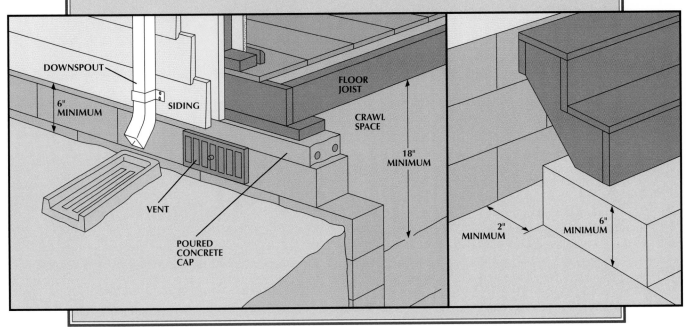

When sealing your house and keeping it clean fail to deter pests, it's time to take more aggressive action. For persistent infestations of rats, bedbugs, ticks, or fleas, call an exterminator. Also enlist a professional to battle insects that threaten structural damage—termites, carpenter ants, or wood-boring beetles. Ridding your house of most other pests is a job you can do yourself. Rodents can be chased out or trapped *(page 104)*. For insect pests, you will probably have to resort to chemicals. First, identify the pest and determine the most effective chemicals to use against it *(pages 105-111)*. Available in many forms, pesticides have a variety of characteristics and applications *(pages 124-125)*.

Space Sprays: Most effective against flying insects, these chemicals kill pests on contact, then break down into harmless by-products within hours. Because they leave no lasting residues, they are often misted into the air of a room from an aerosol can or a fogger—a one-shot aerosol "bomb" that releases its entire contents once activated *(opposite)*.

Residuals: These pesticides may remain potent for weeks, and an insect coming into contact with them may not die until hours later. Commonly available as sprays—and known as surface sprays—these are applied indoors to crevices and other inaccessible areas *(opposite)*; outdoors they create a chemical barrier around the house *(page 103)*. For a large job, you can prepare a solution from a commercial concentrate and apply it with a spray bottle or a garden sprayer.

Residual pesticides are also available in aerosol cans that release their contents as spray or foam. They are also manufactured as paint-on emulsions and as tapes that are applied in small strips in cabinets and around sinks. Some of these products come as fine dusts that work well only in sheltered areas, such as behind walls or in the spaces under the bottom shelves of cabinets. Dusts disperse more widely than sprays and remain potent for months or years.

Baits: This form of pesticide is most commonly available as pellets to kill rats and mice, or as "bait stations" for cockroaches, crickets, earwigs, and ants. Some insect baits are also sold in gel form, and are applied by syringe to the same sites as a residual spray. The pest takes the bait back to its nest or colony and, in many cases, transmits it to other members. The major drawback of baits used against rodents is that the animals may die and decay inside walls, far out of reach.

 TOOLS

	Stud sensor	Putty knife
	Plastic	Sanding block
Spray bottle	squeeze bottle	Spray wand for
Vacuum cleaner	Pressurized	garden hose
Electric drill	garden sprayer	

SAFE PRACTICES WITH PESTICIDES

Pesticides can be poisonous to humans and pets. As with any other chemical, follow label directions—check the safety signal word *(page 10)*—and observe the following precautions:

✓ Never expose food, dishes, food-preparation surfaces, or toilet articles to pesticides.

✓ Do not mist any residual spray into the air or across broad expanses.

✓ If you have small children or pets, keep them out of rooms recently treated with a residual liquid or spray. Use rodent traps rather than poison bait, and place traps, insect baits, or dusts where they will be inaccessible to children and pets.

✓ Many pesticides are flammable; extinguish all flames—including pilot lights and cigarettes—while mixing or applying them. Ventilate a treated room either during or after application, depending on the label directions. To avoid a concentration of vapors, do not use a fogger in a room smaller than the size specified on the label.

✓ Wear nitrile gloves and long sleeves to apply the chemical. Wash thoroughly afterward—and wash immediately if you splash pesticide on your skin. Wear goggles and, when recommended, a respirator with cartridges approved for pesticides.

✓ If you have asthma, hay fever, or allergies, have a professional apply the chemicals.

✓ Store unused portions in the original containers, and keep them and the application equipment in locked cabinets out of children's reach.

✓ Never mix different pesticides.

✓ Keep the container until you have used all the contents. Then, if it held a concentrated liquid, rinse it out three times and add the rinse water to the rest of the product to be applied. Before disposal, puncture and crush nonpressurized containers to prevent reuse; wrap aerosol containers in newspaper.

✓ For a pesticide with active ingredients not listed on pages 124 or 125, call your state's department of agriculture or the EPA to find out whether the substance is approved. If not, ask for disposal instructions.

INDOOR TACTICS

Using a residual spray.

◆ Wearing nitrile gloves, mix the chemical and water in a household spray bottle in the appropriate proportions.

◆ For narrow cracks, set the nozzle to a pin stream; otherwise, use a coarse spray. Alternatively, buy a surface spray in an aerosol can.

◆ Spray cracks, crevices, and narrow surfaces along baseboards, around countertops, and in the corners of cabinets and cupboards. Also treat drawer runners, gaps around pipes, and the floor around appliances. Move the sprayer along the crevice at a rate that leaves a moist film without puddles or pools *(right)*. Put on goggles when spraying overhead.

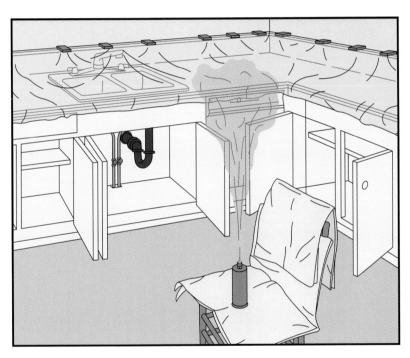

Misting an entire room.

◆ Before setting off an aerosol fogger, turn off pilot lights and extinguish any open flame.

◆ Weight down plastic sheeting over food-preparation surfaces. Cover fish tanks with plastic; turn off fish-tank aerators.

◆ Close doors and windows, and turn off fans and air conditioners. Open cupboards to be treated.

◆ Place the aerosol can on a newspaper-covered chair in the middle of the room and, with the nozzle pointed away from you, press down the discharge tab until it locks in place.

◆ Leave the room promptly and stay out for the prescribed length of time.

◆ Air out the room when you return, and vacuum up the dead insects.

⚠ **CAUTION** *Do not use a fogger in a room that is smaller than the minimum size recommended on the product label.*

TRICKS OF THE TRADE

A Simple Fly Trap

An ordinary glass jar or bottle can be transformed into a highly effective fly trap. For common houseflies, mix 1 part molasses and 3 parts water with a little brewer's yeast, and pour about 1 inch of the liquid into a wide-mouth jar. Twist a piece of paper into a cone, leaving a small hole at the bottom, tape it in this shape, and tape it to the jar with the hole just above the liquid. Place the jar where flies are usually seen, such as on a window sill.

To trap vinegar flies, pour $\frac{1}{2}$ inch of wine into a bottle with a long neck, and place it where flies congregate.

Check traps daily and add water to drown any flies, then empty and refill them.

Applying a dust.

◆ To inject dust under the bottom shelf of a cabinet, drill one $\frac{1}{4}$-inch hole in the cabinet bottom for every 4 to 6 square feet of surface. To treat behind a wall, drill a hole between each pair of studs, 2 or 3 inches from the ceiling.

◆ Unless the product comes in a container with a pointed nozzle, put on a dust mask and nitrile gloves to prepare the dust: pour it into an unused plastic squeeze bottle for mustard or ketchup.

◆ Fit the nozzle of the dispenser into each hole and squeeze it two or three times *(left)*.

◆ Spackle the holes, sand the patches, and touch up the paint.

◆ Wearing a dust mask, also squeeze dust into cracks and crevices and behind appliance kick plates or grilles, applying enough to coat the surfaces with a thin film.

Positioning bait stations.

To control cockroaches, set out bait stations around the perimeter of the infested area at the intervals recommended on the package. Place them behind appliances, furniture, and plumbing fixtures, near garbage cans, on counters, at wall edges, and in cabinets, and pantries *(right)*. Avoid putting them out in the open. Replace the bait stations every three months, or monthly for severe infestations.

To control ants, place the bait stations at the ants' entry points into the house.

BAIT STATION

LAYING DOWN A CHEMICAL BARRIER

Spraying around the house.

◆ Wearing nitrile gloves, goggles, and a respirator with cartridges approved for pesticides, mix a water-base residual pesticide from concentrate in a pressurized garden sprayer.

◆ Holding the wand 8 to 12 inches from the wall, spray the bottom 12 inches of the foundation wall and the first 18 inches of soil against the house *(left)*. Apply enough chemical to wet the wall without dripping or pooling.

◆ If you have a pest problem in the basement, wet down the inside of the window wells.

◆ Apply a 2-inch band of the pesticide across exterior door thresholds and first-floor window sills and about 1 foot up the inside surfaces of door and window frames. Also treat any cracks around door or window frames and below siding.

DESTROYING THE NESTS OF OUTDOOR PESTS

Getting rid of wasp nests.

◆ Purchase a special aerosol wasp spray, designed to shoot a narrow stream 10 to 15 feet.

◆ Wearing nitrile gloves and goggles, and working at dusk with your back to any breeze, direct the stream of pesticide into the nest opening for three to five seconds *(right)*.

◆ Spray the exterior of the nest until the pesticide drips.

◆ After 24 hours—only if there is no sign of activity—knock down the nest and destroy it. Otherwise, repeat the procedure.

⚠ **CAUTION** *Do not spray wasp nests if you are hypersensitive to stings or have asthma, hay fever, or other allergies—have the job done by a professional.*

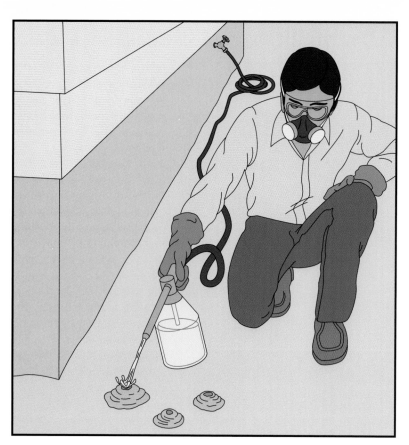

Poisoning an ant hill.
◆ Wearing nitrile gloves, goggles, and a respirator with cartridges approved for pesticides, mix a water-base residual pesticide in a container on a spray wand, as shown, or in a pressurized garden sprayer.
◆ Spray the pesticide into the openings to the colony *(left)* and thoroughly soak the ground around the openings with pesticide—up to several quarts for a large anthill.
◆ Hose down the nest with plain water so the pesticide will be carried deep into the soil.

TRAPPING MICE AND RATS

Setting up a snap trap.
◆ For mice, place peanut butter on the bait pedal; for rats use peanut butter and bacon.
◆ Pull back the bow and secure the locking rod over it.
◆ Carefully holding the trap by its edges—some are strong enough to break a finger—place it with the baited end next to the wall. Position traps every 10 feet along the routes used by the mice or rats.
◆ To protect children and pets from the trap, cut a hole in each end of a cardboard box and set it over the device *(right)*.
◆ If a rodent is killed by the trap, put on gloves and place the used trap and carcass in a heavy-duty garbage bag in an outdoor trash can.

Humane traps *(photograph)* lure a rodent inside and then snap a door closed behind them. The animal can then be released outdoors.

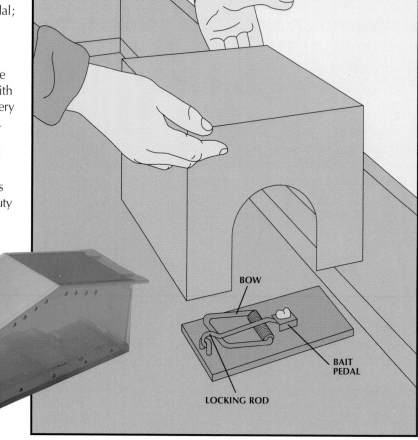

BOW

BAIT PEDAL

LOCKING ROD

To control pests, it is necessary to identify them. Some intruders such as termites and winged ants look very much alike, but are controlled quite differently. It also helps to know pests' nesting and feeding habits and their typical invasion routes so you can follow an appropriate course of action.

A number of pests are profiled in the following pages. Where the recommended control measures include pesticides, use a chemical only if it is suitable for the location; for example, many chemicals cannot be used on bedding.

If you cannot identify an insect, try to capture it in a jar. In most cases, your county agricultural agent can identify it and suggest ways to control it.

Ants.

Most species nest outdoors and find their way into the kitchen, attracted by sweets or grease. A few, however, nest indoors: in a wall cavity, under flooring, or in a pile of undisturbed litter.

Ants generally travel from nest to food source along well-defined paths over window and door sills and along baseboards and countertop edges. Finding these routes will help you control the infestation and locate the nest and destroy it *(opposite)*. For an infestation, apply a residual spray or paint-on preparation along the travel routes; baits may also help. For a heavy invasion from outdoors, create a chemical barrier along the foundation wall with a residual spray *(page 103)*.

Inside, treat any visible nests in the house with a residual spray. For nests inside cavities, apply dust *(page 102)*.

Carpenter ants, black and about $\frac{1}{2}$ inch long, may tunnel into damp wood to nest. Try boring holes and puffing in dust *(page 102)*, or call an exterminator.

Bedbugs.

These $\frac{1}{4}$-inch-long insects inhabit mattresses, sucking blood from sleeping occupants. In severe infestations, they cluster in cracks and crevices throughout the bedroom as well as in seams and tufts in the bedding. Inspect any purchases of used furniture carefully before bringing items home.

To control bedbugs, wet the inside of the bed frame, springs, and slats with a residual spray or paint-on emulsion. Also spray baseboards, cracks between floorboards, and behind wall hangings and loose wallpaper *(page 101)*. With a product specifically for mattresses, spray the seams and tufts very lightly. Complete the treatment by fogging the room with an aerosol *(page 101)*. Do not replace the linens or occupy the room for at least two hours.

⚠️ **CAUTION** *Never spray a baby's crib or bedding with pesticide; instead, wash the bedding and scrub the crib.*

Bees.

Bees are essential to the growth of flowers and fruit, but you may want to get rid of hives that are uncomfortably close to the house. Sometimes a local beekeeper will be willing to adopt a swarm of honeybees. Otherwise, to destroy an outdoor hive, use a wasp spray *(page 103)*; for a hive in a wall cavity, inject dust into the wall above the hive *(page 102)*. After two or three days, remove the hive—even if you must tear away siding or wallboard to do so.

If a swarm of honeybees has settled in shrubbery close to your house, screen or plug all openings under the eaves or into the roof overhang to discourage the swarm from building a hive in these cavities. In dry areas, a gentle shower of water from a garden sprinkler may encourage the swarm to move on; directly spraying the bees, however, will only enrage them.

Although they are not aggressive, carpenter bees become pests by burrowing into exposed timber to nest. To eliminate them, blow dust into the tunnels; several days later, plug the tunnels with caulk.

⚠️ **CAUTION** *Do not try to exterminate bees if you are hypersensitive to stings or suffer from asthma, hay fever, or other allergies—call in a professional.*

Box-elder bugs.

Outdoors, these $\frac{1}{2}$-inch-long, red-banded insects tend to inhabit female box-elder trees. On sunny fall days, they may swarm indoors in great numbers, leaving spots on curtains, clothing, and upholstery. To stem repeated invasions, spray the trees in early summer with a pesticide for controlling aphids, using a pressurized garden sprayer; as a last-ditch measure, you can cut down the trees. During an infestation, a barrier treatment *(page 103)* with a residual pesticide can help. Indoors, fog an infested room *(page 101)*.

Carpet beetles.

Sure signs of infestation are a combination of damaged carpets or upholstery and the appearance of small mottled or black beetles, $\frac{1}{8}$ inch long, crawling near windows. But it is actually the hairy larvae that do the damage, feeding on fabrics as well as furs, stuffed animals, and dried foodstuffs.

If you find carpet beetles or their larvae on your kitchen shelves, treat them in the same way as pantry pests *(page 108)*. Elsewhere, vacuum thoroughly, paying special attention to baseboards, upholstery, drapes, and carpeted areas under furniture and behind radiators. Throw away the vacuum bag; it may contain larvae and eggs. Take small rugs and carpets outside, and brush or shake them. Wash clothes and blankets. Spray a residual pesticide along baseboards, around the edges of carpeting, into cracks between floorboards, at the ends of clothes rods, and around shelves *(page 101)*.

To prevent reinfestation, vacuum frequently and store fabrics properly *(page 94)*.

Centipedes and millipedes.

Most of these pests are intruders from the outdoors, where they thrive in piles of damp leaves, grass cuttings, and compost, and on the damp undersides of boxes and boards resting on the ground. Clear such hiding places from the foundation of your house. If you are plagued by a large number of centipedes, create a chemical barrier around the foundation *(page 103)*.

One species of centipede breeds in the house and can be persistent, although it does no real harm. To control it, coat baseboards and crevices in damp, dark areas—in the basement, kitchen, and bathroom, and in closets—with a residual spray *(page 101)*.

Clothes moths.

You are unlikely to see a clothes moth—these $\frac{1}{4}$-inch-long insects shy away from light—but you will find evidence of them in the damage done by their larvae to carpets, upholstery, blankets, and clothing. Clothes moths prefer fur and wool, but they will feed on synthetics if the fabric is dirty or stained. Clothes moths are controlled in the same way as carpet beetles. Vacuum often and store clothes and other fabrics properly *(page 94)*.

Cockroaches.

Universally abhorred, cockroaches earn their reputation by contaminating food, soiling walls and counters, causing allergies, and possibly spreading disease. To control them, begin in the kitchen, usually the area of severest infestation—clear off counters, empty cabinets, and spray a residual pesticide into cockroach hiding places *(page 101)*. Then puff a dust across floor areas under appliances, into the spaces under cabinets and, in a severe infestation, into the walls behind appliances *(page 102)*. Finally, fog the room *(page 101)*. Once the pesticide is dry, cover shelves with shelf paper to protect dishes and food from the chemical's residual effects.

To control cockroaches in a living room or bedroom, spray a residual pesticide lightly into crevices on the underside of furniture, around pictures and hangings, and along baseboards, ceiling moldings, and the edges of shelves. Set off an aerosol fog if the infestation is heavy. In a bathroom, spray a pesticide into cracks and gaps where it will not be quickly washed away. A second treatment with a residual spray may be needed two to four weeks later, as a new generation of cockroaches emerges from eggs that survived the first treatment. A month after spraying, place bait containers near cockroach hiding places *(page 102)*.

Fleas.

Loathed for their irritating bite, fleas can hitchhike into your house on a pet, then spread. First, treat the pet, following the advice of a veterinarian, and launder pet bedding in very hot water. In infested rooms, vacuum rugs, curtains, upholstery, and all areas under and behind furniture and radiators; then throw away the vacuum bag. Spray a residual pesticide *(page 101)* into cracks between floorboards, along baseboards, behind loose wallpaper, in crevices on the undersides of furniture and, lightly, into the seams and tufts of upholstery. Also spray crevices in the box or basket in which the pet sleeps with a spray recommended for this application. Then fog the room with a flea bomb containing a growth regulator, which prevents larvae from developing into adult fleas. For outdoor control, spray doghouse cracks and crevices with an indoor sprayer. With the spray attachment of a garden hose, soak the pet's favorite resting places with a residual spray. Let the product dry before letting the pet into the yard.

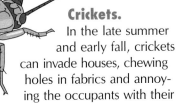

Crickets.

In the late summer and early fall, crickets can invade houses, chewing holes in fabrics and annoying the occupants with their chirping. If large numbers are entering, create an exterior barrier with a residual pesticide *(page 103)*. Indoors, apply a residual spray *(page 101)* along baseboards and the bottoms of walls in all rooms in which you have seen or heard crickets; be thorough in basements and closets and on the floors under stairwells. Also spray the floors of unused fireplaces. If the infestation is heavy, fog the room to chase the insects into the residual pesticide *(page 101)*.

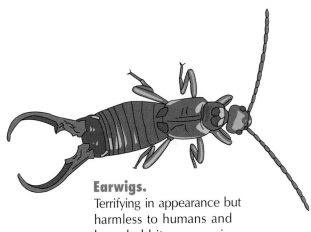

Earwigs.

Terrifying in appearance but harmless to humans and household items, earwigs usually haunt moist, shady areas of the yard under wood and tangled shrubbery. Occasionally, however, they make their way indoors, sometimes crawling into piles of laundry and bedding. A barrier treatment with a residual pesticide *(page 103)* will stem an invasion. Indoors, spray along baseboards and the bottoms of walls wherever you have seen earwigs *(page 101)*. Also put out bait stations in areas where you have not sprayed *(page 102)*.

Flies.

Sound window screens and snug-fitting screen doors that swing outward are the best defense against houseflies. Sanitation in the kitchen and the yard *(pages 94-95)* will also reduce their numbers. If maggots appear in a garbage can, wash the can thoroughly with hot water and detergent. In a room overrun with flies, treat it with a space spray *(page 101)*, but do not expect more than temporary control. Flypaper gives longer-lasting but less complete protection. To deal with only a few flies, try a homemade jar trap *(page 101)*.

Mites.

Two species of mites, both barely visible to the unaided eye, are common household pests. The clover mite *(right)* can invade the house in great numbers from a lush, well-fertilized lawn, leaving reddish smears on walls and floors whenever it is crushed. Cut back grass and shrubs from exterior walls, and spray the foundation with a residual spray *(page 103)*. Indoors, fog the infested areas *(page 101)*, then vacuum them and throw away the bag.

The house-dust mite inhabits cotton-stuffed mattresses, pillows, and upholstery, and sometimes triggers violent allergies. Vacuum carpets, mattresses, furniture, and floorboard cracks, and keep the house well ventilated to avoid the moisture buildup that mites favor.

Mosquitoes.

In warm weather, tiny mosquito larvae will breed in any standing water around the house—in puddles in the yard, on a flat roof, or in a clogged rain gutter. Indoors, look for larvae in fish tanks and in the saucers under houseplants. Drain any infested water. For a persistent mosquito problem in a backyard fish pond, stock larvae-eating fish such as goldfish, guppies, mosquito fish, or sticklebacks.

To bar mosquitoes from indoors, keep screens tight-fitting and in good repair. You can temporarily rid a room of mosquitoes with an aerosol fog *(page 101)*.

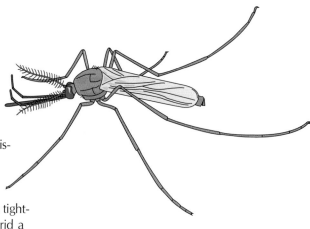

Pantry pests.

Dry food can attract many different types of beetles, as well as the larvae of several moth species, which feed on grains, cereals, dry soup mixes, dried fruits, nuts, cocoa, pet food, and spices. The most common of these insects is the sawtoothed grain beetle *(right)*.

Pantry pests most often get into homes in groceries. If you see beetles or wormlike larvae in a new package of dry food, dispose of it immediately. If the package has been on your shelves for some time, destroy it; then empty the shelves, vacuum them, and seal uninfested food in jars, coffee cans, or plastic bags with a zip-locking top. If no infestation is visible, but you suspect it, spread the food in a baking pan in a 140°F oven for 30 minutes or place it in the freezer for several days.

For a heavy infestation of pantry pests, spray or paint a residual pesticide *(page 101)* around the edges of the shelf. Let the pesticide dry and, to avoid contaminating the food, apply shelf paper before restocking the shelves.

Scorpions.
Abundant in the South and Southwest, scorpions can deliver a painful—and sometimes fatal—sting. Indoors, they lurk in many of the same areas favored by spiders *(below)*; you may also spot them in a bathroom or a kitchen sink, where they search for moisture. Outdoors, they hide in piles of wood and trash, and they may burrow into a child's sandbox. Control them as you would spiders.

Silverfish.
Silverfish range throughout the house, doing minor damage to paper, bookbindings, wallpaper, starched fabrics, and rayon. Control them with a residual spray *(page 101)* applied to baseboards, along the bottoms of walls, and around pipe chases. Also treat closets in rooms where you have seen silverfish. For a severe infestation, inject dust under cabinets and into walls *(page 102)*. Spray again two weeks later to kill silverfish that hatch from eggs unaffected by the first treatment. Similar in appearance to the silverfish, and sometimes confused with it, the firebrat frequents areas near heat sources, such as radiators, hot-water pipes, ovens, and furnaces. Do not use sprays in these locations, which could present a fire hazard; instead, puff dust under and behind radiators and hot-water pipes, under and around ovens and furnaces, and in all baseboard crevices in warm areas.

Sowbugs.
Sowbugs and a related species, pillbugs, are similar in appearance and size ($\frac{1}{4}$ to $\frac{1}{2}$ inch). Both are harmless and prefer the same damp habitats as centipedes. Control them as you would centipedes *(page 106)*.

Spiders.
Undisturbed areas in closets and under and behind furniture can shelter spiders. Most are harmless, but two species are dangerous: the black widow *(right)*, with its characteristic red or brown spot on the underside; and, in the South, the brown recluse, distinctively marked on the top with a dark brown spot shaped like a violin. A poisonous spider in a living room or bedroom is usually a casual intruder from an unkempt yard or a cluttered garage or basement. Where possible, clear away piles of lumber, boxes, and debris stored indoors or out. Wear gloves and a jacket as you work, and watch for spiders, their webs, and their $\frac{1}{2}$-inch-long silken egg sacs. Vacuum up or destroy the webs, and stamp on the egg sacs.

A barrier treatment of a residual pesticide *(page 103)* may reduce the number of spiders invading from outdoors. Indoors, apply a residual spray *(page 101)* along baseboards and in corners wherever you have seen spiders.

Termites.

These pests feed on wood and can cause severe structural damage to a house. In an area favorable to termites, take measures to keep them at bay *(page 99)*. Getting rid of termites is usually a job for a professional exterminator, but be alert for signs of infestation. In the early spring, a swarm of winged insects emerging from the soil near the foundation, or from wood inside or outside the house, is a sign of trouble. If the insects have long forewings and short hindwings, they are winged ants; on winged termites, both pairs are the same length. Termites also have thicker waists and straight, not bent, antennae. Another clue is the mud-walled shelter tubes through which termites travel from their underground nests to their sources of food, typically leading up concrete foundation walls to the wood framing above. If you see blisters or dark areas on wood floors or paneling, probe them with a screwdriver or an awl; if the wood is infested, your tool will easily sink into the damaged timber.

A few termite species reveal their presence with piles of small, brown fecal pellets on the floor under infested wood. Common along the Gulf and Pacific coasts, they nest in the house rather than underground, and build no shelter tubes.

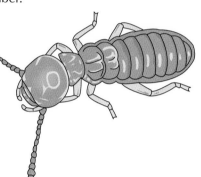

Ticks.

Brown dog ticks are the kind that most often invade houses. They generally arrive in the fur of dogs, then drop off and lay their eggs in carpets, upholstery, cracks between floorboards and behind baseboards, and the spaces behind loose wallpaper. Brown dog ticks do not bite humans, but other species that do may infest yards in summer. Ticks are controlled in much the same way as fleas *(page 107)*. Wash pet bedding in very hot water. Indoors, apply a residual pesticide as for flea control, and fog the room with an aerosol flea bomb. In the yard, follow the directions for flea control *(page 107)*. Have a veterinarian treat the dog.

Wasps.

Many wasps anchor their nests in bushes or trees or under eaves. Hornets and yellow jackets *(below)* build paperlike football-shaped nests; umbrella wasps construct honeycombed paperlike nests shaped like an umbrella canopy;

and mud daubers build chambered nests of mud. Other wasps, including some yellow jackets, tunnel into the ground to nest. Destroy any wasp nest that is uncomfortably close to your house with a special spray *(page 103)*. Yellow jackets occasionally nest inside walls. Drill a hole into the wall above the nest, and puff dust into the wall cavity; then plug the hole. For a very large nest inside a wall, or one that dust does not destroy, summon professional help. Some wasps build nests underground. For these species, wait until nightfall, then blow two or three puffs of dust into the nest opening with a squeeze bottle. Immediately cover the entrance with a shovelful of moist earth.

> ⚠️ **CAUTION** *Do not try to exterminate wasps if you are hypersensitive to stings or suffer from asthma, hay fever, or other allergies; call in a professional.*

Wood-boring beetles.

The most common wood-boring beetles—powder-post beetles *(right)*, deathwatch beetles, furniture beetles, and old-house borers—can attack any wood in the house but are most likely to infest hardwood flooring, paneling, furniture, and framing. Signs of their presence are the oval holes that adult beetles leave as they emerge from the wood in which they have developed and, on the floor beneath the holes, small heaps of sawdust. Control is a matter for professional exterminators, but you can discourage the most common wood-boring beetles by keeping your crawl space well ventilated and dry. Firewood stored outdoors may harbor beetles; stamp on any you see scuttling out of the wood when you bring it into the house.

Bats.

Bats may nest in attics or sheds, or in the cavities at the top of a concrete-block wall. The odor of their urine and guano can be a nuisance. To get rid of a stray bat or two nesting in an attic, screen off their access routes while they are out for the night, using $\frac{1}{4}$-inch or finer mesh *(page 96)*; be sure young bats have not remained inside. If a few bats are nesting in a concrete-block wall, pour moth crystals into the cavities to drive them out. Then close off the cavities or the gaps that gave them access to the wall. For large infestations, call a professional.

Mice.

Some mice live in buildings year-round, destroying foodstuffs, fabric, paper, and wood; others move in from the outdoors when the weather turns cold. A small mouse can slip through a $\frac{1}{4}$-inch hole, so seal all gaps in exterior walls *(pages 97-98)*, especially near the top of the foundation wall. Eliminate indoor mice with traps *(page 104)* or poison bait.

Rats.

Feared as disease carriers, rats are best controlled by cleanliness. Order and sanitation in the yard *(page 95)* will deprive rats of shelter and nesting areas. You can further discourage them by storing lumber, pipes, and boxes at least a foot above the ground, on racks or supports, to make them inaccessible for nesting.

Keep rats out of the house by plugging any opening larger than $\frac{1}{2}$ inch on foundation walls or siding *(pages 97-98)*. Use concrete patching compound, sheet metal, or hardware cloth for sealing, depending on the surrounding material. Roof rats, common in the South and along the Pacific coast, can also enter buildings under the eaves; to keep them out, plug gaps high on the siding as well.

If rats venture indoors, snap traps *(page 104)* may help you cope with them; if this strategy isn't successful, try poison bait.

EVICTING BIRDS AND SMALL ANIMALS

When a single chipmunk, squirrel, bat, or bird strays into your house, put on a jacket and heavy work gloves to protect your arms and hands from bites, then shoo it out the way it came in, urging it along with a broom. Chipmunks or squirrels that have moved into the attic or basement can be captured and released outdoors with humane traps; inquire at the local humane society. If birds have built a nest in a chimney or a roof vent, wait until the fledglings have left, then push out the nest and screen off the spot. For a potentially dangerous animal such as a raccoon, porcupine, or skunk, call the police or animal-control center for assistance.

⚠ **CAUTION** *Do not go near an animal that seems ill or unafraid—it may be rabid. Leave the area immediately and call local authorities for assistance.*

Appendix

5

The success of any cleaning task depends on using the right product and method. The charts in this section will help you select those that are appropriate for treating waxed wood floors, metals, fabrics, and swimming pools. You'll also find information on choosing effective pesticides.

Cleaning Hardwood Floors **113**

Restoring Metal Surfaces **114**

Caring for Fabrics **116**

Cures for Stained Textiles **118**

Treating Swimming-Pool Water **122**

Choosing Pesticides **124**

CLEANING HARDWOOD FLOORS

For spots on wood floors with a surface finish, such as polyurethane, wipe the area with a rag dampened in a detergent or vinegar solution. If the finish is damaged, patch the spot or refinish the floor.

A number of substances, as listed in the left-hand column of the chart below, can mar the surface of waxed hardwood floors. Cleaning methods for each type are provided on the right, listed in order of effectiveness and harshness. Start with the gentlest method, progressing to stronger ones only if the stain lingers.

Removing the blemish will likely also strip the wax; if it does, rewax the spot. When using steel wool, apply very light pressure to avoid removing the finish under the wax; if rubbing thins the finish, patch it (page 17).

Ventilate the area well when using chemical cleaning agents. With chlorine bleach and lye soap, wear rubber gloves; for ammonia, add goggles. Mineral spirits requires nitrile gloves and goggles. When cleaning with trichloroethylene, put on goggles and PVA gloves.

Problem	Cleaning Methods
Alcohol spots	Rub with a cloth dipped in liquid or paste wax.
Black heel marks, caster marks	Rub with #3/0 steel wool dipped in floor wax; buff or let dry according to label directions.
Burns	Rub with #3/0 steel wool.
Chewing gum, crayon, candle wax, tar	Apply ice to harden, then scrape off with dull knife. Remove residue with #3/0 steel wool dipped in mineral spirits or trichloroethylene.
Dried food	Rub with a damp cloth, then wipe dry.
Ink stains	Rub with #1 steel wool dipped in mineral spirits. Sand with medium-grit, then fine-grit sandpaper. Apply a 1:32 solution of oxalic acid and water.
Mold, mildew	Rub with a cloth dipped in chlorine bleach; wipe with a cloth dipped in plain water; dry thoroughly.
Oil, grease	Rub with lye soap, then rinse. Saturate a cotton cloth with hydrogen peroxide and place over stain; then saturate a second cloth with ammonia and place over the first.
Scuffs, scratches	Buff the affected area. Rub with #3/0 steel wool dipped in paste wax; wipe off excess, and buff.
Urine stains	Clean as for ink; replace the board if this doesn't work.
Water spots	Rub with #2/0 steel wool. Sand lightly with fine-grit sandpaper. Rub with #1 steel wool dipped in mineral spirits.

RESTORING METAL SURFACES

The cleaning agent and methods you use on metal will depend on whether the surface is unfinished, painted, or coated with lacquer. The chart below lists cleaners and techniques for most types of metal surfaces. Liquid detergent or a commercial cleaner formulated for the particular metal will sometimes be all you need. Cleaning tips and cautions that apply to certain metals are listed in the last column on the right. Aluminum siding has a factory-applied enamel finish. Clean it in the same way as wood siding *(page 15)*.

When working with lacquer thinner or a metal polish, ventilate the area. Wear rubber gloves to apply metal polish; nitrile gloves for lacquer thinner, and add goggles to protect your eyes from splashes. To prevent spontaneous combustion of a cloth soaked with lacquer thinner, hang it outdoors to dry or store it in an airtight metal or glass container until you can dispose of it safely.

UNFINISHED METAL

Surface	Cleaning Agent	Cleaning Method	Tips and Cautions
Aluminum	Mild liquid detergent and warm water; for tough dirt, baking soda and water	Wash with a soft cloth or brush dampened in cleaner, then rinse; dry with a soft cloth. For screens, scrub with a soft brush and hose off; rap with your hand to shake off water and allow to dry.	Avoid abrasive pads and cleaners. Do not use ammonia.
Brass, bronze, copper	Commercial brass polish	Apply polish with a soft cloth, let dry, then buff with a soft cloth.	Remove especially heavy tarnish with stripping solution *(page 29)*.
Chrome	Mild liquid detergent and warm water; for mineral deposits, full-strength vinegar	Wash with a cloth or sponge dampened in cleaner, then rinse; dry with a soft cloth. For mineral deposits, rub with a soft cloth dampened in vinegar. On heavy deposits, leave on a vinegar-soaked cloth for several hours.	Avoid abrasive pads and cleaners.
Pewter	Commercial pewter or brass polish	Apply polish with a soft cloth and let dry; buff with a soft cloth. Wash with mild liquid detergent and warm water, then rinse; dry with a soft cloth.	Avoid harsh abrasives. For tough spots, rub gently with fine steel wool dipped in olive oil.

Surface	Cleaning Agent	Cleaning Method	Tips and Cautions
Silver	Mild liquid detergent and hot water; commercial silver polish	Wash, rinse, and dry silver. Apply polish with a soft cloth; rub polish off with a soft cloth. Rinse and dry again.	A small toothbrush is useful for crevices, chased surfaces, and beaded edges. Wash off all traces of polish.
Stainless steel	Mild liquid detergent and hot water	Wash with a soft cloth dampened in cleaner, then rinse; dry with a soft cloth.	On brushed finishes, rub out scratches with #3/0 steel wool, working with the grain. On highly polished finishes, avoid abrasive pads and scouring powders.

FINISHED METAL

Surface	Cleaning Agent	Cleaning Method	Tips and Cautions
Lacquered metal	Mild liquid detergent and warm water	Wash gently with a soft cloth dampened in solution, then rinse; dry with a soft cloth.	Avoid cleaners and metal-polishing compounds containing abrasives or ammonia. Remove old lacquer with hot vinegar used at full strength or commercial lacquer thinner.
Painted metals indoors *appliances, radiators, doors*	Mild liquid detergent and warm water	Vacuum to remove dust, then wash with a cloth or sponge dampened in cleaner; rinse, then dry with a soft cloth.	Avoid cleaners containing abrasives or ammonia. Commercial appliance polish protects painted surfaces.
Painted metals outdoors *railings, gates, fences*	Mild liquid detergent and warm water	Wash with a soft-bristle brush dampened in solution, then rinse.	Remove rust using a drill fitted with a wire-brush attachment *(page 32)*; for heavy jobs, use a sandblaster *(page 32)*. Protect cleaned metal with rust-resistant primer and paint.

CARING FOR FABRICS

Where labels on clothing or household fabrics include care instructions, always follow those directions. Otherwise, base your cleaning method on the fiber from which the item is made. The chart below lists common fibers, and the suggested cleaning methods for each type. If the composition of the article is not indicated on a label, how the article is used may help you determine what it is made of. Many fabrics are blends of different fibers. When dealing with such a fabric, you will likely have to choose between different cleaning methods. Always opt for the gentlest. For example, polyester can be machine-washed and dried, but acetate must be dry-cleaned or hand-washed and drip-dried. There-

Fiber	Uses	Recommended Care
Acetate	Bed linens, drapes, upholstery, clothing	Dry-clean or hand-wash in warm water. Drip dry; do not wring or twist. Iron while damp, on wrong side, at low setting. Do not use acetone.
Acrylic	Blankets, carpets, drapes, upholstery, knitted clothing	Hand-wash delicate weaves; for others, machine wash in warm water. Use fabric softener with every fourth washing to prevent static cling. Machine-dry at low heat; iron at low setting. Avoid direct sunlight and lay flat to dry.
Cotton	Bed linens, towels, carpets, drapes, upholstery, clothing	Machine-wash woven fabrics in warm water and machine-dry at warm setting. To reduce shrinkage, wash in cold water and hang to dry. Do not use full-strength chlorine bleach. Iron at high setting.
Linen (flax)	Table linens, upholstery, clothing	Machine-wash whites in warm water. Dry-clean or hand-wash colored fabrics. Iron at high setting.
Fiberglass	Curtains, drapes	Hand-wash in warm water, wearing rubber gloves and goggles. Drip-dry; no ironing necessary. Never machine wash.
Modacrylics	Awnings, blankets, carpets, drapes, synthetic furs, sleepwear	Machine-wash in warm water; use fabric softener. Machine-dry at low heat; iron at low setting. Dry-clean synthetic furs. Do not use acetone.
Nylon	Bed linens, carpets, drapes, upholstery, clothing	Machine-wash in cool to warm water; wash colored fabrics separately. Use only nonchlorine bleach. Use fabric softener with every fourth wash to prevent static cling. Machine-dry at low heat; iron at low setting.

fore, when cleaning a polyester/acetate blend, treat it like acetate to avoid damaging its acetate fibers. Other considerations in caring for a fabric are its weave, and its dyes and finishes. The label will usually tell you what you need to know; some will indicate, for example, that the article can be dry-cleaned only. When labels are absent, follow common sense. For example, use a gentle wash cycle for loosely woven and knit fabrics. When ironing textured fabrics such as wool crepe, use only light pressure.

Although stain removal often calls for special cleaners (pages 118-121), some fibers can be damaged by certain products; do not use acetone solvents, for example, on acetate fibers.

Fiber	Uses	Recommended care
Olefin	Carpets, carpet backings, upholstery, underwear, sportswear	Dry-clean or machine-wash in lukewarm water. Machine-dry at low heat—do not use a gas-fired commercial dryer. Do not iron 100 percent olefin; iron olefin blends at lowest setting.
Polyester	Bed linens, carpets, curtains, drapes, cushion stuffings, clothing	Dry-clean or machine-wash in warm water; use fabric softener every third wash. Wash colors separately. Machine-dry at low heat; iron at low setting.
Rayon	Bed linens, table linens, carpets, curtains, drapes, upholstery, clothing	Dry-clean or hand-wash in lukewarm water. Do not twist or wring; iron at low setting. Do not use full-strength chlorine bleach.
Silk	Bed linens, table linens, carpets, drapes, clothing	Dry-clean or hand-wash gently in cold water. Use only neutral or non-alkaline detergent. Use nonchlorine bleach only; do not twist or wring. Iron at low setting. Do not dry in direct sunlight.
Spandex	Athletic clothing, bathing suits, lingerie	Dry-clean or machine-wash in lukewarm water. Use nonchlorine bleach. Machine-dry at low heat. Iron at low setting.
Triacetate	Drapes, upholstery, clothing	Machine-wash in warm water. Machine-dry at medium heat. Iron at high setting. Do not use acetone.
Wool	Blankets, carpets, upholstery, clothing	Dry-clean or hand-wash in lukewarm water. Use only neutral or nonalkaline detergent. Do not use chlorine bleach. Do not wring or twist. Dry flat; iron at low setting with steam. Do not dry in direct sunlight.

CURES FOR STAINED TEXTILES

For most fabric stains, there are one or more stain-removal agents with the ability to remove it *(chart below and pages 119-121)*. To use the chart, scan the left-hand column to find the substance that caused the stain. Then, moving right, use the stain-removal agent indicated with the number "1": First check that the agent is safe for the fabric *(pages 116-117)*. If the product is safe, test it on an inconspicuous spot *(page 48)*, and then work on the stain as described on pages 49 to 51. If the stain-removal agent is not safe for the fabric or the spot remains, try the next cleaner in the chart.

Most stains are based on either protein from animal sources such as eggs, milk, and blood; or tannin from plants such as coffee, tea, or tomatoes. Stains that are not listed in the chart can be treated like others in the same category.

Where detergent is recommended, mix it with an equal volume of water. If detergent with ammonia or vinegar is specified, apply the detergent, then add a few drops of the vinegar or ammonia.

For an enzyme presoak product—used to treat stains before laundering—mix it according to the package directions, or use a detergent containing enzymes.

Substance	Dry-cleaning fluid	Amyl acetate	Acetone	Water	Detergent	Detergent and ammonia	Detergent and vinegar	Enzyme presoak product	Rust remover	Detergent and ammonia	Bleach	Dye remover
Adhesive tape	1											
Asphalt	1				2	3	4		5		6	
Bath oil	1											
Beer				1	2		3		4		5	
Beets				1	2		3		4		5	
Berries				1	2		3		4		5	
Blood				1	2	3	4				5	
Butter	1			2	3	4						
Candy				1	2		3		4		5	
Chocolate				1	2		3		4		5	
Coffee				1	2		3		4		5	
Corn syrup				1	2		3		4		5	
Cough syrup				1	2		3		4		5	
Crayon	1			2	3	4	5		6		7	
Deodorant				1	2						3	
Dye (fabric)				1	2		3		4	5		6
Egg (white and yolk)				1	2	3		4			5	
Excrement				1	2	3		4			5	

When using bleach, you can apply any type that is safe for the fabric. For chlorine bleach, mix 1 part bleach with 4 parts water, and do not leave the solution on the fabric for longer than two minutes before rinsing it out. For sodium perborate and sodium percarbonate bleach, mix 1 teaspoon with 4 ounces of water. Hydrogen peroxide (3 percent) can be used full strength. Hydrogen peroxide, sodium perborate, and sodium percarbonate can be left on a fabric for up to 15 minutes.

To prepare a dye remover, mix 1 teaspoon in 4 ounces of water and leave it on the fabric for no more than 15 minutes. For a rust remover, buy a product formulated for laundry and mix it according to package directions; or, use oxalic acid, diluting 1 tablespoon in 2 cups of water.

Amyl acetate, acetone, dry-cleaning fluid, vinegar, and ammonia are used full strength.

Whichever cleaning agent you use, ventilate the work area well, and wear goggles if there is any chance of splashing the cleaner in your eyes. Put on rubber gloves when working with acetone, ammonia, dye remover, rust remover, or bleach. Amyl acetate requires nitrile gloves.

Substance	Cleaning Agent											
	Dry-cleaning fluid	Amyl acetate	Acetone	Water	Detergent	Detergent and ammonia	Detergent and vinegar	Enzyme presoak product	Rust remover	Detergent and ammonia	Bleach	Dye remover
Fish slime				1	2	3		4			5	
Food color				1	2		3		4	5		6
Fruit juice				1	2		3		4		5	
Glue (solvent-base)	1	2	3									
Glue (yellow, white)				1	2	3						
Grass	1	2		3	4		5		6		7	
Gravy	1				2	3	4	5	6		7	
Grease (food)	1				2	3	4					
Grease (machine)	1				2	3	4					
Gum	1	2	3									
Hair coloring				1	2		3		4	5		6
Hair spray	1				2	3	4					
Ice cream				1	2	3		4			5	
Ink	1				2	3	4	5	6		7	
Jam, jelly				1	2		3		4		5	
Ketchup				1	2		3		4		5	
Lacquer	1	2	3									
Lard	1				2	3	4					

Substance	Dry-cleaning fluid	Amyl acetate	Acetone	Water	Detergent	Detergent and ammonia	Detergent and vinegar	Enzyme presoak product	Rust remover	Detergent and ammonia	Bleach	Dye remover
Lipstick	1			2	3	4	5		6		7	
Liqueurs and spirits				1	2		3		4		5	
Makeup: blush	1			2	3	4	5		6		7	
Makeup: eye liner, shadow	1			2	3	4	5		6		7	
Makeup: foundation	1			2	3	4	5		6		7	
Makeup: mascara	1			2	3	4	5		6		7	
Maple syrup				1	2		3		4		5	
Margarine	1			2	3	4						
Mayonnaise	1			2	3	4	5		6		7	
Meat juice				1	2	3		4			5	
Mildew				1	2						3	
Milk				1	2	3		4			5	
Molasses				1	2		3		4		5	
Mucus				1	2	3		4				
Mud				1	2	3						
Mustard	1			2	3		4		5		6	
Nail polish	1	2	3									
Oil (cooking)	1			2	3	4						
Oil (motor)	1			2	3	4						
Paint (latex and oil)	1			2	3	4	5		6		7	
Paint (watercolor)				1	2		3		4	5		6
Pencil				1	2	3						
Perspiration				1	2	3		4			5	
Rust									1			
Scorching				1	2						3	
Shaving cream				1	2							
Shellac	1	2	3									

Substance	Dry-cleaning fluid	Amyl acetate	Acetone	Water	Detergent	Detergent and ammonia	Detergent and vinegar	Enzyme presoak product	Rust remover	Detergent and ammonia	Bleach	Dye remover
Shoe polish (liquid)	1	2		3	4	5	6		7		8	
Shoe polish (wax)	1			2	3	4	5		6		7	
Smoke	1			2	3	4	5		6		7	
Soft drinks				1	2		3		4		5	
Solder	1	2	3									
Soot	1			2	3	4	5		6		7	
Soy sauce				1	2		3		4		5	
Sun screen	1			2	3	4	5		6		7	
Tar	1			2	3	4	5		6		7	
Tea				1	2		3		4		5	
Tobacco				1	2		3		4		5	
Tomato				1	2		3		4		5	
Toothpaste				1	2							
Urine				1	2	3		4			5	
Varnish	1	2	3									
Vomit				1	2	3		4			5	
Wax (candle)	1			2	3	4	5		6		7	
Wax (floor, automobile)	1			2	3	4	5		6		7	
White correction fluid	1	2	3									
Wine				1	2		3		4		5	

MYSTERY STAINS

For a blemish of unknown origin, first remove any surface buildup with a dry brush, then try a spot test with dry-cleaning fluid *(page 48)*. If it causes no damage, perform the cleaning steps on pages 49 to 51. When dry-cleaning fluid is not safe for the fabric or the stain lingers, repeat the process with these cleaners in order until the stain is gone: detergent; detergent and vinegar; detergent and ammonia; and bleach—provided bleach is safe for the fabric *(pages 116-117)*.

TREATING SWIMMING-POOL WATER

Many of the water-quality problems that beset swimming pools can be corrected by adjusting either the filtration system or the water's chemical balance (chart, below and opposite). Some remedies require checking the pH and chlorine levels of the water with a test kit (page 80) and, if necesssary, adding the appropriate chemicals to correct a problem. To deal with water hardness and total alkalinity, you need special test chemicals, available in kit form at pool-supply stores. The water-hardness test indicates whether there is excessive calcium in the water. The alkalinity test reveals total alkaline content in the water—which should range from 80 to 150 parts per million—indicating whether the pH is out of balance.

Problem	Possible causes	Treatment
Cloudy water	Too-frequent back-washing of sand filter	Do not backwash the filter until the pressure gauge reads 10 psi above normal.
	Clogged or torn filter elements	Check the filter elements in a cartridge filter; replace damaged elements. Add a degreaser to the elements. Monitor the pressure gauge; backwash promptly when it reaches 10 psi above normal.
	Dirt particles too fine to be trapped in filter	Add coagulant to the pool to clump dirt particles. Monitor the pressure gauge closely to prevent dirt from clogging the filter. Backwash promptly when pressure reads 10 psi above normal.
	High pH	Check and correct the pH level. Test pH daily until it is stabilized.
	Chalking paint (concrete pool)	Repaint the pool every 3 years.
Water turns blue, brown, or black when first treated with chemicals	Chlorine combining with metals—iron, copper, manganese—to form minute particles	Check and correct the pH level. Add a sequestering agent. Then run the filter continuously to remove metallic sediment, checking the pressure frequently and backwashing as needed. Vacuum out any sediment remaining in pool.
Standing water turns green, reddish brown, or black. Dark blotches and slippery spots form on walls.	Green algae	Superchlorinate, concentrating treatment in areas of visible algae growth. Run the filter continuously for 6 to 8 hours, checking the pressure frequently and backwashing as needed. Vacuum any remaining algae from pool surfaces. Check and correct the pH level. Add an algae inhibitor.
	Black algae	Scrub algae spots with a wire brush to expose growth buds. Turn off the filter. When water is still, superchlorinate, concentrating chlorine near areas of growth. Restart the filter after 6 hours. Brush and vacuum dead algae from pool sides and bottom. Check the filter pressure frequently; backwash as needed. Check and correct the pH level. Add an algae inhibitor.
	Mustard algae	Place all pool tools in water for treatment. Superchlorinate; adjust the pH level to between 7.4 and 7.6. Brush algae from pool walls and add a special algicide designed for mustard algae to the pool. Run the filter continuously until water is clear, backwashing as needed. Vacuum any remaining algae from pool surfaces.

Other chemical correctives listed in the treatment column of the chart—such as algae inhibitor, coagulant, degreaser, sequestering agent, and antiscale solution—are sold in pool-supply stores; refer to the labels for dosages. When superchlorination is recommended, you need to add calcium hypochlorite to the water—1 pound for every 10,000 gallons of water—every two weeks until the chlorine level drops below 3.0 parts per million (ppm). Undertake this treatment at a time when the pool will not be used for at least 6 hours. Some treatments involve running the filter continuously and backwashing *(pages 82-83)*. When working with pool chemicals, follow the safety guidelines on page 79.

Problem	Possible Causes	Treatment
Foamy water	Excess algicide	Add fresh water to dilute the concentration. Test the chlorine and pH levels frequently until readings are normal.
Chlorine odor	Nitrogen compounds in pool water reducing chlorine efficiency	Superchlorinate; check and correct the pH level. Thereafter, check and correct the chlorine and pH levels more frequently.
Stained pool walls	Low pH and low total alkalinity	Test total alkalinity; increase it to an acceptable level by adding sodium bicarbonate to pool. Check and correct the pH level with pH booster.
Corroded pipes and fittings	Low pH and low total alkalinity	Treat as for stained pool walls.
Etched pool surfaces	Low total alkalinity and insufficient dissolved calcium	Test the total alkalinity; increase it to acceptable levels by adding sodium bicarbonate to pool. Use calcium carbonate to increase calcium hardness.
Scaling on pool surfaces, filter, water-heating hardware	High total alkalinity and high calcium hardness	Test the total alkalinity; reduce it to acceptable levels by adding muriatic acid or sodium bisulfate to pool. Check and correct the pH level as necessary. Add an antiscale solution to filter tank.
Erratic and rapidly changing pH levels	Total alkalinity out of balance	Test the total alkalinity. If it is too low, increase it to an acceptable level by adding sodium bicarbonate to the water. If the total alkalinity is too high, lower it by adding hydrochloric acid or sodium bisulfate.

CHOOSING PESTICIDES

The label on a pesticide is an important guide. It provides a roster of insects against which it is effective and the ingredients *(chart below, left)*, which determine the chemical potency of the product, as well as any hazards associated with its use. The label also describes how a pesticide should be used. In the case of residual sprays and paint-on preparations, for example, the Environmental Protection Agency (EPA) specifies the areas of a house to which the substance may safely be applied *(chart below, right)*. This information provides a clue to the product's toxicity. In general, substances limited to use in cracks, crevices, and areas such as joints around baseboards are more toxic and long-lasting. Chemicals that can be sprayed over larger surfaces such as the insides of cabinets and areas under furniture are less toxic and leave shorter-lived residues. Only certain products can be safely applied to pet bedding. Whatever the potency of a pesticide, follow the general precautions on page 100 and wear the appropriate safety gear when using it *(pages 101-104)*.

Before applying a pesticide, test it on an inconspicuous part of the surface to be treated—some products can stain or mar certain surfaces.

Common name	Forms used	Duration of effect	Comments and cautions for indoor use
Boric acid	Dust	Effective as long as it is undisturbed.	Effective only against crawling insects; ineffective when wet. Unlike many pesticides, does not repel insects and drive them into hiding. Often placed in wall voids during construction for lasting protection. Although a common household chemical, boric acid is a poison.
Brodifacoum	In rodent baits	Effective indefinitely.	Effective against rats that are resistant to warfarin. Poisonous to humans and pets, but only in large amounts.
Chlorpyrifos	Residual spray, paint-on emulsion	Residue from spray lasts 15-30 days; paint-on form is effective for months.	An all-purpose pesticide, effective against a wide range of insects. Apply only to cracks, crevices, and small areas. Strong smelling.
Diazinon	Residual spray, dust	Residue from spray lasts 15-30 days; dust is effective for months.	An all-purpose pesticide, effective against a wide range of insects. Apply only to cracks, crevices, and small areas. Will damage ferns, hibiscus, and gardenias.
D-phenothrin	Residual spray, space spray, dust	Residue lasts 1-15 days.	See resmethrin.
D-trans allethrin	Space spray, residual spray	Residue lasts 1-15 days.	See resmethrin.
Hydramethylonon	Bait stations and gel baits	Effective for more than 30 days.	Effective against cockroaches and ants.
Hydroprene	Space sprays, residual sprays	Residue lasts 90-180 days.	Effective against cockroaches and fleas.

Common name	Forms used	Duration of effect	Comments and cautions for indoor use
Methoprene	Space sprays and residual sprays	Residue lasts for more than 3 months.	Effective against ants, mosquitoes, and fleas.
Naphthalene	Balls, flakes	Gives off repellent vapors for months.	Primarily used to mothproof woolens, but only moderately effective. Repels small animals such as bats. Has a penetrating odor.
Paradichlorobenzene	Balls, flakes	Gives off repellent vapors for months.	See naphthalene.
Permethrin	Space sprays, residual sprays, dusts	Residue lasts 1-15 days.	See resmethrin.
Propoxur	Residual spray, bait, resinated tape	Residue from spray and tape lasts 15-45 days; bait is effective indefinitely.	An all-purpose pesticide effective against a wide range of insects. Apply only to cracks, crevices, and small areas. Gives out penetrating vapors.
Pyrethrins	Space spray, dust	Residue lasts minutes to hours.	As a space spray quickly stuns and kills flying insects and flushes out and kills crawling insects. Breaks down quickly once applied. Can cause allergic reactions in some people. Toxic to fish.
Resmethrin	Space spray, residual spray	Residue lasts 1-15 days.	As a space spray, effective against most flying and exposed insects. As a residual spray, effective against most crawling insects. Toxic to fish. Can cause allergic reactions in some people, but less so than pyrethrins.
Silica gel	Dust	Effective as long as it is undisturbed.	Effective against crawling insects, but ineffective when wet.
Tetramethrin	Space sprays, residuals	Residue lasts 1-15 days.	See resmethrin.
Tralomethrin	Space sprays, residuals	Residue lasts 1-15 days.	See resmethrin.
Warfarin	In rodent baits	Effective indefinitely.	Mixed with meal or grain to poison rats and mice; sometimes several doses are needed. Poisonous to humans and pets, but only in large amounts.

INDEX

Acetate fabrics: 9, 10, 116
Acetone: 9, 118-121
Acid safety: 21
Acrylics: 33; countertops, 36; fabrics, 116; skylights, 37; storm windows, 35
Alcohol: on fabrics, 120; on wood, 14, 113
Alcohol as a cleaner: 9
Aluminum, cleaning: 29, 115
Ammonia: 9, 10, 113, 118-121
Amyl acetate: 118-121
Ants: 100, 104, 105, 124, 125
Appliances: 64-74, 91
Asphalt driveways: 25
Asphalt stains: 22, 118
Attic vents, pestproofing: 96

Baking soda: 10
Bathtubs: 9
Bats: 111, 125
Bedbugs: 100, 105
Beer: 118
Bees: 105
Beetles: 100, 106, 108, 110
Beets: 118
Berries: 118
Birds: 111
Bleach: 8, 10, 113, 116, 117, 118-121
Blinds: 31
Blood: 118; on masonry, 22
Box elder bugs: 106
Brass: cleaning, 29, 115; sealing, 30
Brass stains on masonry: 22
Bricks: 20-21, 26-28
Bronze, cleaning: 115
Bronze stains on masonry: 22
Brooms: 10
Buffers, wax: 18
Burns on wood floors: 113
Butter: 118

Candy: 118
Carpets: cleaning, 52-53, 56-57, 91; pet stains, 51; raising depressions, 53; repairing, 57-58
Caulk removal from masonry: 22

Ceilings: 42-43
Centipedes: 106
Chandeliers: 39
Chemical safety: 10, 21, 79
Chimneys, pestproofing: 96
Chipmunks: 111
Chocolate: 118
Chrome: 10, 115
Cleaners: 8
Clothes: cleaning, 91, 116-117; stain removal, 46, 48-51, 118-121
Clothes dryers: 64, 71-72
Clothes washers: 64, 71, 91
Cockroaches: 102, 107, 124
Coffee stains: on fabrics, 118; on masonry, 22; on porcelain and tile, 41
Concrete: 21, 24
Cooktops: 64, 66-67, 69-70
Cookware: 9
Copper, cleaning: 29, 115
Copper stains: on masonry, 22; on porcelain, 9
Corn syrup: 118
Correction fluid: 121
Cotton fabrics: 116
Cough syrup: 118
Countertops: 36
Crayon: on fabrics, 118; to fill scratches, 36; on wood floors, 113
Crickets: 107

Degreasers: 14
Deodorant stains: 118
Detergents: 8, 114-115, 118-121
Dishwashers: 64, 74, 91
Disposal of cleaners: 8
Drains, clogged: 10
Driveways: 24, 25
Dry cleaning fluid: 8, 118-121
Dry sponges: 42
Dusters: 11; for blinds, 31
Dust mops: 11
Dye removers: 118-121
Dyes: 118

Earwigs: 107
Efflorescence: 9, 21
Eggs: 118
Electricity safety: 84-85
Electrolysis: 30

Enzyme-containing products: 51, 118-121
Excrement: 51, 118

Fabrics: cleaning, 116-117; stain removal, 46-51, 118-121
Fans: 90, 91
Fiberglass, polishing: 33
Fiberglass fabrics: 116
Filters: in air conditioners, 76; in furnaces, 77-78; for pools, 82-83; in range hoods, 75; water filters, 40
Finishes, identifying: 13, 16
Fish: 119
Flammable-product safety: 10
Fleas: 100, 107, 124, 125
Flies: 101, 108
Floods: 84-91
Floors: tile, 10; vinyl, 10, 33-34; wood, 9, 16-18, 113
Food coloring: 119
Foundations, pestproofing: 97, 99
Freezers, cleaning: 64
Fruit juice: on fabrics, 119; on porcelain, 41
Furniture: 13-14, 19, 91. See also Upholstery

Garbage disposers: 64, 73
Glass: 10, 37-39
Gloves: 10, 22
Glue: 9, 119
Goggles: 10
Grass stains: 119
Gravy: 119
Grease: 8; on concrete, 21; on fabrics, 9, 47, 119; on masonry, 22; on porcelain and tile, 41; on wood floors, 113; on woodwork, 14
Grout: 40, 41
Gum: 8; on fabrics, 48, 119; on masonry, 22; on wood floors, 113

Hair products: 119
Hard-water scale: 10, 41, 74
Heel marks: 41, 113
Hydrogen peroxide: 113, 117

Ice cream: 119
Ink: on fabrics, 9, 119; on masonry, 22; on wood floors, 9, 113; on woodwork, 14
Insects: 105-108, 109, 110, 124, 125
Iron, cleaning: 29, 32
Ivy stains: 20

Jam: 119
Jeweler's rouge: 23, 35

Ketchup: 119
Kettles, cleaning: 10

L

Lacquer removal: 9, 119
Ladder safety: 37
Laminates: 33, 36
Lard: 119
Leather furniture: 61
Linen: 116
Lipstick: 120
Liqueurs: 120
Liquids, wicking: 47
Lye soap: 113

M

Makeup: 120
Maple syrup: 120
Margarine: 120
Masonry: 9, 22; asphalt, 25; bricks, 20-21, 26-28; concrete, 21, 24; power washers, 26-28; stone, 22-24
Mayonnaise: 120
Meat stains: 120
Metal: after flooding, 91; cleaning, 29-32, 114-115
Metallic stains: on masonry, 22; on natural-fiber fabrics, 10
Mice: 104, 111, 125
Microwave ovens: 64, 68
Mildew: 120; on porcelain and tile, 41; on siding, 15; on wood floors, 113
Milk: 120
Millipedes: 106

Mineral oil: 14
Mineral spirits: 14, 113
Mites: 108
Modacrylic fabrics: 9, 116
Molasses: 120
Mold on wood floors: 113
Mops: 11
Mosquitoes: 108, 125
Mothballs: 125
Moths: 106, 108, 125
Mucus: 120
Mud: 120
Muriatic acid: 9, 83
Mustard: 120

Nail polish: 9, 120
Nylon fabrics: 116

Oil: on concrete, 21;
    on fabrics, 118, 120;
    on porcelain and tile, 41;
    on wood floors, 113
Olefin fabrics: 117
Orange oil: 8
Organic solvents: 8
Ovens: 64, 68, 70
Oxalic acid: 9, 113

Paint removal: from fabrics,
    120; from masonry, 20, 22;
    from porcelain and tile, 41;
    from woodwork, 14
Pencil stains: 120
Perchloroethylene (PERC): 8
Perspiration: 9, 10, 120
Pesticides: 100-104, 105,
    124-125
Pestproofing homes: 94-99
Pests: 105-111, 124, 125
Pet stains: 51
Pewter, cleaning: 29, 115
Phosphates: 8
Pillbugs: 109
Plastic on concrete: 21
Plastics, cleaning: 33-36
Poison safety: 10
Polishing: acrylic storm
    windows, 35; finished
    wood, 13; metals, 29,
    30, 115; stone, 23;
    vinyl floors, 33-34;
    waxed floors, 18

Polyester fabrics: 117
Pools: 79-83, 122-123;
    chemical safety, 79
Porcelain: 40, 41
Porcupines: 111
Poultices: 9, 22
Power washers: 26-28
Pressure wands: 15
Pressure washers: 26-28
Pumice: 14

Rabid-animal safety: 111
Raccoons: 111
Ranges: 64, 66-70
Rats: 100, 104, 111, 124, 125
Rayon fabrics: 117
Refrigerators: 64, 65-66
Respirators: 10
Rodents: 100, 104, 111,
    124, 125
Rottenstone: 14
Rugs: cleaning, 52, 54-55, 91;
    stain removal, 46-51
Rust on metal: 32
Rust removers: 118-121
Rust stains: on fabrics, 120;
    on masonry, 9;
    on porcelain, 9, 41;
    on sinks, 9, 10; on tile, 41;
    preventing stains, 40

Safety equipment: 10
Safety precautions: acids, 21;
    bees, 105; chemicals, 10, 21;
    flammable products, 10;
    ladders, 37; pesticides,
    100, 105; poisons, 10;
    pool chemicals, 79; rabid
    animals, 111; spontaneous
    combustion, 30; wasps,
    103; water and electricity, 84
Sandblasting: 32
Sanding: acrylics, 35, 36;
    stone, 23
Scale removal: 10
Scorching: 120
Scorpions: 109
Scouring pads: 12
Scrapers, razor-blade: 37
Scratches: on acrylics, 35, 36;
    on laminates, 36; on stone,
    23; on wood floors, 113
Scrub brushes: 12
Shaving cream: 120

Shellac: 120
Shoe polish: 121
Siding, cleaning: 15
Silicone sealers: 24
Silk fabrics: 117
Silver, cleaning: 29, 30, 115
Silverfish: 109
Sinks: 9, 10, 40, 41
Skunks: 111
Skylights: 37
Smoke: 121
Soap scum: 41
Sodium bicarbonate: 10
Soft drinks: 121
Solder: 121
Solvent safety: 30
Solvents, organic: 8
Soot: 121
Sowbugs: 109
Soy sauce: 121
Spandex fabrics: 117
Spiders: 109
Spontaneous combustion: 30
Squeegees: 25, 37-39, 87
Squirrels: 111
Stainless steel: 29, 115
Stain removal: 46-51;
    from fabrics, 118-121;
    from masonry, 20-22;
    from woodwork, 14
Steel wool: 14, 113
Stone: polishing, 23; rust
    stains, 9; sanding
    scratches, 23; sealing, 24
Sun screen: 121
Swimming pools: 9, 79-83,
    122-123

Tape, removing: 8, 43, 118
Tar: on fabrics, 121; on
    masonry, 22; on wood
    floors, 113
Tarnish: 29, 30, 115
Tea stains: on fabrics, 121;
    on masonry, 22;
    on porcelain and tile, 41
Termites: 99, 100, 110
Testing cleaners: 48, 52
Textiles: cleaning, 116-117;
    stain removal, 46-51, 118-121
Ticks: 100, 110
Tile: 9, 10, 40, 41
Tin oxide: 23
Tobacco stains: on fabrics, 121;
    on masonry, 22
Tomato stains: 121

Tools: 11-12, 15, 18, 25, 37,
    38, 52
Toothpaste: 121
Trash compactors: 64, 73
Triacetate fabrics: 9, 117
Trichloroethylene: 22, 113
Tung oil: 30

Upholstery: cleaning, 59-61;
    stain removal, 46-51,
    118-121
Urine: on carpets, 51;
    on fabrics, 9, 10, 121;
    on wood floors, 113

Vacuum cleaners: 12;
    for pools, 81; upholstery
    attachments, 61
Varnish removal: 9, 121
Vinegar: 10, 118-121
Vinyls: blinds, 33; floors, 10,
    33-34; furniture, 61;
    siding, 33
Vomit: on carpets, 51;
    on fabrics, 121

Wallpaper: 42
Walls, exterior: pestproofing,
    98, 99, 103;
    power washing, 26-28
Walls, interior: 42-43;
    removal after flooding, 89-90
Wasps: 103, 110
Water-damaged items: 84-91
Water spots: on wood floors,
    113; on woodwork, 14
Wax buildup: 14
Waxed floors: 16-18
Wax stains: 113, 121
Wicker furniture: 19
Wicking: 47
Windows: 35, 37-39
Wine: 121
Wood, cleaning: 13-18, 113
Wool fabrics: 117

TIME® LIFE BOOKS

Time-Life Books is a division of Time Life Inc.

TIME LIFE INC.
PRESIDENT and CEO: George Artandi

TIME-LIFE BOOKS
PRESIDENT: John D. Hall
PUBLISHER/MANAGING EDITOR:
Neil Kagan

HOME REPAIR AND IMPROVEMENT:
Cleaning
EDITOR: Lee Hassig
MARKETING DIRECTOR: James Gillespie
Deputy Editor: Esther R. Ferington
Art Director: Kathleen Mallow
Associate Editor/Research and Writing:
  Karen Sweet
Marketing Manager: Wells Spence

Vice President, Director of Finance:
  Christopher Hearing
Vice President, Book Production:
  Marjann Caldwell
Director of Operations: Eileen Bradley
Director of Photography and Research:
  John Conrad Weiser
Director of Editorial Administration:
  Barbara Levitt (Acting)
Production Manager: Marlene Zack
Quality Assurance Manager: James King
Library: Louise D. Forstall

ST. REMY MULTIMEDIA INC.
President and Chief Executive Officer:
  Fernand Lecoq
President and Chief Operating Officer:
  Pierre Léveillé
Vice President, Finance: Natalie Watanabe
Managing Editor: Carolyn Jackson
Managing Art Director: Diane Denoncourt
Production Manager: Michelle Turbide

Staff for Cleaning

Series Editors: Marc Cassini, Heather Mills
Series Art Director: Francine Lemieux
Art Director: Michel Giguère
Assistant Editor: Rebecca Smollett
Designers: Jean-Guy Doiron, Robert Labelle
Editorial Assistant: James Piecowye
Coordinator: Dominique Gagné
Copy Editor: Judy Yelon
Indexer: Linda Cardella Cournoyer
Systems Coordinator: Éric Beaulieu
Other Staff: Linda Castle, Lorraine Doré

PICTURE CREDITS
Cover: Photograph, Robert Chartier. Art, Michel Giguère. Steam cleaner provided by Bissell Ltd.

Illustrators: Jack Arthur, Gilles Beauchemin, George A. Bell Jr., Frederic F. Bigio (B-C Graphics), Edward L. Cooper, François Daxhelet, Roger Essley, Adsai Hemintranont, William Hennessy Jr., Elsie J. Hennig, Walter Hilmers Jr. (HJ Commercial Art), John Jones, Arezou Katoozian (A and W Graphics), Dick Lee, François Longpré, John Martinez, John Massey, Joan McGurren, Eduino J. Pereira (Arts and Words), Jacques Perrault

Photographers: **End papers:** Glenn Moores and Chantal Lamarre. **10, 15, 19, 25, 31, 37, 38, 42, 58, 61, 101, 104:** Robert Chartier. **18:** Oreck Corporation. **52:** Bissell Ltd. **81 (top):** Rainbow Lifeguard Products Inc. **81 (bottom):** Kreepy Krauly USA. **91:** Minuteman International Inc.

ACKNOWLEDGMENTS
The editors wish to thank the following individuals and institutions: American Association of Poison Control Centers, Washington, DC; Amway Corporation, Ada, MI; Elaine Andrews, University of Wisconsin Environmental Resource Center, Madison, WI; Association of Specialists in Cleaning and Restoration, Annapolis Junction, MD; ATP Results Inc., Monroe, LA; Bissell Ltd., Niagara Falls, Ontario; Brick Institute of America, Reston, VA; Canadian Conservation Institute (Department of Canadian Heritage), Ottawa, Ontario; The Carpet and Rug Institute, Dalton, GA; Chemfree Environment Inc., Kirkland, Quebec; Ron Conner, Connor's Pool and Spa, San Antonio, TX; Crain Tools, Milpitas, CA; Dello Sbarba Inc., Montreal, Quebec; Don Aslett's Cleaning Center, Pocatello, ID; Michel Farell, Verdun, Quebec; Fedders Corporation, Liberty Corner, NJ; D. Douglas Fratz, Chemical Specialties Manufacturers Association, Washington, DC; GE Appliances, Louisville, KY; Louis V. Genuario, Genuario Construction Company Inc., Alexandria, VA; Gilmour Manufacturing, Summerset, PA; Hoover Canada, Burlington, Ontario; Lloyd Hudson, Crossville Ceramics, Bedford, TX; Inter-Mares Trading Co., Inc., Lindenhurst, NY; Jacuzzi Brothers, Division of Jacuzzi Inc., Little Rock, AR; Kreepy Krauly USA, Sunrise, FL; Master Force Marketing Inc., Owatonna, MN; Paul McGoldrick, Pianoforte, Montreal, Quebec; Minuteman International Inc., Addison, IL; The National Institute of Restoration Inc., Charlottesville, VI; National Oak Flooring Manufacturers Association, Memphis, TN; National Wood Flooring Association Inc., Manchester, MO; New York Wicker and Rattan, New Rachell, NY; NuTone, Cincinnati, OH; Wanda Olson, University of Minnesota Department of Design, St. Paul, MN; Omni Corporation, Hammond, IN; Marshall Oreck, Oreck Corporation, New Orleans, LA; Painting and Decorating Contractors of America, Fairfax, VA; Piscine RF Gilbert Inc., Chateauguay, Quebec; Porcelain Enamel Institute, Nashville, TN; Prosol Distribution Inc., St-Laurent, Quebec; Rainbow Lifeguard Products Inc., Elmonte, CA; Society of American Silversmiths, Cranston, RI; Target Products, Kansas City, MO; United Abrasives Inc., Willimantic, CT; The Vinyl Institute, Morristown, NJ; Fred Waller, Raleigh, NC; Wetmore & Associates Ltd., Park Forest, IL; Winsow Laboratories, Seattle, WA; Wood Floor Covering Association, Anaheim, CA

Library of Congress Cataloging-in-Publication Data
Cleaning / by the editors of Time-Life Books.
  p. cm. — (Home repair and improvement)
Includes index.
ISBN 0-7835-3908-8
1. House cleaning.
I. Time-Life Books. II. Series.
TX324.C58 1997
648'.5—dc21   96-37921